CHARACTER COUNTS
FOR ATHLETES
VOLUME 3

Rod Handley and Gordon Thiessen

ISBN 1-929478-68-2

Cross Training Publishing
317 West Second Street
Grand Island, NE 68801
(308) 384-5762

Copyright © 2004 by Cross Training Publishing

Unless otherwise indicated, all Scripture quotations are from the *Holy Bible, New International Version,* © 1973, 1978, 1984, International Bible Society.

This book is manufactured in the United States of America.

Library of Congress Cataloging in Publication Data in Progress.

CONTACTING THE AUTHORS

Character Counts for Athletes Volume 3

Rod Handley
512 NE Victoria Drive
Lee's Summit, MO 64086
816-525-6339
www.characterthatcounts.org

Gordon Thiessen
Cross Training Publishing
P.O. Box 1541
Grand Island, NE 68802
1-800-430-8588
www.crosstrainingpublishing.com

Please contact us to purchase this or any of our other volumes (1 and 2) that teach character qualities.

The authors want to thank the following sports ministries for their partnership on this project. Detailed information about each of them is found at the back of this book.

*Fellowship of Christian Athletes
*Church Sports and Recreation Ministers
*Athletes in Action

CONTENTS

PREFACE BY ROD HANDLEY

We're living in perilous times in the 21st century. Every day we see, hear and experience numerous situations that point out a tremendous character shortage in society. It would be easy for believers to exclude themselves from this character crisis. But the sad reality is that many Christians fall woefully short of exhibiting character and integrity to a watching world.

Charles Edward Jefferson wrote a classic book in 1907 entitled, *The Character of Jesus* which has become one of my all-time favorites. Listen to what he said about his generation, "There are others of us who are discontented, not so much with ourselves as with the world. The time is out of joint, and we are sick at heart because no one seems to be wise or strong enough to set it right. Government is corrupt, the church seems dead or dying, the home is a failure or scandal, society is superficial and tainted, the social order is ready for the burning, the economic system is a burden and curse, the whole framework of the world needs to be reconstructed." Jefferson's comments are remarkable....if I didn't know otherwise, I would've thought he was talking about today.

Like Jefferson, I subscribe that the only person who is capable of addressing this grim situation is Jesus Christ. Christ was the perfect manifestation of every single character quality. As believers we have access to the King of Kings in helping us be a godly leader and truly living out a life of character. This book is dedicated to Jesus Christ and to the writings of Charles Jefferson. Every chapter features one of Christ's character qualities and then shows us how we can follow His example.

This book is designed for personal use or for doing with a group of other believers. Enjoy the journey in building your character.

BROTHERLINESS

BE A FRIEND THAT STICKS CLOSE

BROTHERLINESS: Exhibiting a kinship and disposition to render help because of a relationship.

Call it Camp Cunningham. Former Philadelphia Eagles quarterback Randall Cunningham, coming back after missing most of the prior NFL season because of knee surgery, paid the expenses to fly four of his favorite receivers to Las Vegas for a week of workouts. Cunningham spent more than $30,000 for air fare, expenses, equipment and rental of the field, office space and gymnasium in order to reacquaint himself with his key teammates. One of the receivers commented, "I've never heard of anybody doing something like this before."

1. What qualities do you look for in a friendship?
2. How do most people choose their friends?

Within each of us, whether or not we want to admit it, there lies a deep desire to have a true brother or sister in our lives. As the oldest of four siblings, I treasure my family relationships, but what I'm talking about here goes beyond genetic connection. Brotherliness is a sense of kinship and a disposition to render help, based on a relationship which offers assistance, no matter the cost or consequences. Kinship is tied to the concept of "we are family," extending beyond immediate family.

Jesus Christ modeled this trait, making a profound impression on both his friends and foes. His enemies sneered that He was a friend of tax collectors, prostitutes and sinners, but Jesus was not deterred. He was friendly and brotherly even to the lowest of society. Jesus not only spoke to these people but he ate with them, went into their homes and sat down to the table with them; the very climax of audacity! In spite of what some believed, they too, were members of the human race, children of the great family of God. Therefore, in spite of all that they had done, and recognizing all that they were, Jesus treated them as brothers.

Throughout the Gospels, Jesus spent time with individuals from many different backgrounds with unique needs. One common denominator in these relationships is His spirit of brotherliness. Jesus sought opportunities to minister to people through a listening ear, a touch or a challenge. Three specific examples in the book of John demonstrate the depth and breadth of His ability to connect as a brother. In spite of their differences, each had needs which only Christ could meet.

First, Jesus interacted with Nicodemus, who represented the best of the Jewish nation, in John 3:1-21. Nicodemus was a highly respected teacher, a member of the Sanhedrin and a Pharisee. His encounter with Jesus was a polite, theological discussion which has a clear brotherly tone. In their lively dialogue, Jesus explained the whole concept of being "born again." Though we don't see the specific results of this visit, we have indications based on later references (John 7:50-51 and John 19:39-40) that something very significant happened to Nicodemus that night.

Then, in John 4:1-26, Jesus engaged in conversation with a Samaritan woman at the well. Their meeting was by chance. Initially this despised, immoral woman was hostile and very shocked that Jesus would even talk to her, but Jesus captured her attention and stimulated her curiosity. He established communication bridges by taking the time to listen and build rapport; His questions aroused her interest. Without being obnoxious, the truth emerged as Jesus turned the conversation to her spiritual needs. The outcome was that this woman was converted, witnessed to her friends and brought other people to belief in Christ.

Finally, in John 5:1-15, Jesus met the need of a paralytic. The invalid at the Bethesda well laid helplessly for 38 years without one single friend, when all he needed was a lifting hand. Jesus' brotherliness is clear in his treatment of the sick. He performed many miracles of healing. He couldn't look upon the deaf and dumb, the palsied, the blind, without putting forth his power to help them.

1. Have any of your friends stuck with you closer than a brother? Describe.
2. What does it mean to be open and honest with your friends? What does it mean to accept one another? Give examples.
3. It has been said, "If you want a friend, be a friend." What does this mean?

Brotherliness was also manifested in Jesus' teachings. He had compassion for people. He saw their confusion, their perplexity and their misery. He saw sheep without a shepherd, and His heart cried out for them. He said, "Come to me and I'll give you rest." It was the moan of a brotherly heart. Jefferson tells us, "Without brotherliness there can be no religion that is pleasing unto God." In spite of all the ugliness, vindictiveness and maligning—He went on helping them all He could. And when they laid their plots to kill Him, he bravely went forward, proclaiming that His death would convince them that He was their brother.

Although many of us have numerous friends and acquaintances, the brotherliness Christ demonstrated is rare in today's world. John 15:13 defines true friendship by telling us, "Greater love has no one than this, that one lay down his life for his friends." In our fast paced world, we often become consumed with schedule, agenda, job, life and reputation-- missing chances to live out brotherliness. Ministry leaders, pastors and full-time Christian workers have numerous opportunities to engage this character quality every day, but many don't pursue it. Why? Such reasons include lack of time, a desire to maintain privacy, mistrust of others primarily due to past hurts, a fear of rejection, a secret pattern of sin and an unwillingness to change and get help, just to name a few.

In the early 1990's, Jimmy Swaggert confessed when his struggles with sexual sin became known throughout our nation. He said, "I fasted and I prayed and I begged God for deliverance from pornography. I realize now if I had turned to my brothers in Christ for help, I would have been delivered." The help that Jimmy needed was sitting in his congregation each and every week, yet he didn't realize the importance of his brotherly relationships until after his embarrassing patterns were exposed.

Dr. Howard Hendricks stated, "Those who are serious about living a pure and effective life before the Lord will find more strength when accompanied by true brothers." Each one of us needs brothers or sisters that will help us in our pursuit of godly behavior. In Ecclesiastes 4:9-10 we are told, "Two are better than one, because they have a good return for their work. If one falls down, his friend can help him up. But pity the man who falls and has no one to help him up!" Real brothers are attentive. They don't miss opportunities to help you because they are aware of your needs.

We violate one of God's basic principles when we try to exist without brotherly relationships. True brothers not only stand with us and sharpen us, but they are also willing to confront us. Hebrews 3:13 reminds us, "But encourage one another day after day, as long as it is still called 'Today,' so that none of you will be hardened by the deceitfulness of sin." I'm not naturally a confrontational guy, but I recognize that if I'm going to grow in depth and maturity, I need brothers who are willing to honestly share the truth with me by pointing out my blind spots, by asking me the hard questions, by challenging me and praying for me. David Augsburger commented, "Life without confrontation is directionless, aimless, passive. When unchallenged human beings tend to drift, to wander, to stagnate. Confrontation is a gift. Confrontation is a necessary stimulation to jog one out of mediocrity or to prod one back from extremes."

I'm at my best when I'm operating with a team of people around me, people who are committed to sharpening me. Ted Engstrom once remarked, "About the only thing we can do successfully by ourselves is fail." My track record shows that my failure rate is significantly higher when I face life alone. Therefore, I actively pursue brotherly relationships, and it's my desire to be a brother to those who need me as well. These intentional friendships are men who are my soul mates. People I would die for and those who would be willing to die for me as well.

Brotherliness is where the rubber hits the road. As Jefferson so well states, it was the distinguishing mark of Jesus' ministry because it validated His work. How are you doing? Do you have true brothers and sisters in your life? Are you being a true brother or sister to someone who needs you?

1. Answer the questions as noted in the final paragraph above.

2. Read Proverbs 27:5-7 and Ecclesiastes 4:9-12. How do these verses apply to friendships? Give some examples.

3. Share a time when you laid your life down for a friend or when a friend laid down his life for you.

This week, write out and memorize Proverbs 18:24

CANDOR

CANDOR: Speaking the truth at the time when the truth should be spoken.

A.C. Green is one of my favorite all-time athletes because he stood up for his beliefs by announcing, "I'm going to remain a virgin until I get married." As a former chaplain for the Seattle SuperSonics, I saw first hand the temptations available to professional athletes before and after each game. A.C.'s stance was rare. It made him a target and a prize for some ladies so A.C. took appropriate precautions. He made sure he followed up his words with an accountability structure. In each city, he had people identified to assist him to and from the airport, the team hotel and the arena. These people provided protection from the potential perils which awaited him. A.C.'s candor, coupled with the pursuit of accountability, allowed him to be victorious.

1. What does it mean to be a person committed to "candor?"
2. Why is it important for people to be candid?

We live in a society that strives to be politically correct, and because we desire to not offend others with our words or actions, we often walk on eggshells. Taking a stand and communicating our convictions is increasingly rare in today's society, even for Christians.

What is lacking is straight talk or "candor." The definition of candor is "to become white or bright." In modern speech, it means "openness, fairness, outspokenness and sincerity." Jefferson tells us that candor is one of the most winsome virtues. He says, "Many people don't possess it. Most of us are reserved and secretive. Our heart isn't open--there are barred lips and a bolted heart. It's possible to be respected and admired but not loved. Jesus was loved. Men loved him so intensely they were willing to die for him. Why? He had an open heart sharing honestly about himself."

Jesus has a great love for people who exhibit candor, as displayed in His interaction with Nathaniel, a citizen of Cana. Philip desired to bring Nathaniel to see Jesus, but Nathaniel's response was, "Can there be anything good out of Nazareth?" Cana and Nazareth were bitterly jealous communities, and Nathaniel had a deep-seated contempt for dingy little Nazareth. Philip continued to simply say, "Come and see." Although he was cynical, Nathaniel went to investigate himself. He had his presuppositions and prejudices, but he wasn't enslaved by them; he had an open mind and an ingenuous heart. When Jesus spotted Nathaniel he was impressed and exclaimed, "Behold an Israelite indeed, in whom is no guile." No craft or cunning, no duplicity or deceit. Here was a man of frank sincerity, and Jesus' heart immediately turned to him.

In contrast, Jesus grew increasingly frustrated with the Pharisees because of their hypocritical behavior. The Pharisees were con men, wearing masks to hide their real personalities. Jesus constantly told them, "Don't be hypocrites." On occasion he called them "vipers." It was a harsh word, yet it accurately expressed their venomous and deadly spirit. With the Sadducees, Jesus repeatedly told them they were ignorant both of the Scriptures and the power of God.

As Christians, we can learn from Jesus' example of not holding back the truth when it needed to be spoken even with those we dearly love. With the twelve disciples, Jesus warned of the terrible risks and dangers associated with being a disciple. In Matthew 10 he tells them they are going out as a "sheep among wolves." He paints a very bleak picture. The only encouragement he gives them is the promise that one day he will confess them before his Father in heaven. His candor reduced the number of his followers. Even in John 2, at the wedding feast he chastised his mother when he said, "Woman, what have I to do with you?" There were times when wounding words had to be spoken.

1. Describe a time when you have stood up for your beliefs and convictions in the face of possible persecution. What ultimately happened?
2. Why are people afraid to speak out against the world, which is promoting sexual promiscuity, addictive behaviors and inappropriate conduct?

The Gospel writers documented these great confessions of Jesus, and Jefferson remarks, "The New Testament is like its hero, gloriously candid. Nothing inspires confidence in a man like candor. If a man is frank and honest in nine points, you can trust him in the tenth." You can trust him because of his open heart.

Jesus didn't water down words. He spoke the truth, holding nothing back. Since Jesus is so frank and open with us, why should we not be open-hearted and frank with him and others? Remember though, being frank does not mean being hurtful. Candor is honest communication delivered with care and concern, not righteousness.

Genuine Christians desire to live for Jesus Christ and obey him. However, temptations are real and powerful, and our flesh, sin nature and Satan himself constantly challenge our faith. No person has the ability to always make the right decisions. Today, our churches and ministries are littered with examples of men and women who have had visible public failures, destroying many loved ones as their secret sin was exposed. The stark reality is that none of us, including myself, are exempt from stumbling, and as Christians we all need accountability in our lives.

Accountability. People are afraid of the word. Perhaps it's because many are unwilling to develop close, intimate friendships or answer to anyone. This is especially true for those in leadership positions. We are taught to be efficient, goal-oriented, disconnected from people, unemotional and self-sufficient, and we can articulate many reasons for not being involved with an accountability partner--including lack of time, a desire to maintain privacy, mistrust of others primarily due to past hurts, fear of rejection, and secret patterns of sin, just to name a few. But we are kidding ourselves if we think we can run the Christian race of faith alone. Scripture shows us clearly that God designed us to be in relationships with one another. Certainly there are times when we must walk alone and be a bright, shining light to the world when possibly no one else will join us. Yet, we each need a person of refuge who is committed to helping restore, equip and teach us to walk in the path God has set before us.

So what is accountability? Being accountable means being responsible and answerable to someone. It means committing yourself on a regular basis (I suggest weekly) to get real with people of the same sex and ask the hard questions of one another. It involves not only having a confidante point out your blind spots and aggressively work with you on your personal character development, but also stand by you and rejoice during the good times as well. It means owning up to past hurts and present shortcomings by committing to positive change. It begins with seeing the need to make changes and having the courage to make it happen with a new plan of action. Every person needs protection from self, along with a safety net. That net is your accountability partner.

Some of us are veterans when it comes to accountability relationships, but we need to be vigilant and speak with as much candor as our counterparts who are just beginning. One of the dangers within an established accountability group is the members becoming so comfortable with one another that they gloss over sin and sin patterns. If you find your partner/group sharing the same issues from week to week without actively challenging one another and seeking Jesus' direction in addressing those issues, you may need to regroup. On the other hand, if you know that your accountability partner(s) are actively listening and your conversations are sometimes difficult due to the candor of your dialogue, you are working toward greater depth in your relationship with Jesus Christ and your Christian brothers and sisters.

Do you desire to become a man or woman of candor? Jesus displayed it beautifully in his own life. We are called to raise the standard and do so in ours as well. Join an accountability group— you'll not regret it!!

1. What does Jesus' candor mean to you? What can we learn from his example?
2. What goes through your head when you hear the word "accountability?" What excites you and scares you about becoming accountable?
3. Are you currently in an accountability group? If so, tell the others about your accountability partner(s) and what you do when you're together. If you don't have an accountability group, would you be interested in starting one? Why or why not?
4. How would accountability in your life help you show more candor?

This week, write out and memorize Proverbs 27:17

COURAGE

BRAVERY AND HEROISM AT ITS BEST

COURAGE: Fulfilling my responsibilities and standing up for convictions in spite of being afraid.

In 1994, University of Texas freshman kicker Phil Dawson had a spectacular year. As a result, he was named to Playboy Magazine's Preseason All-American football team. As a Christian, Dawson took a stand and told the magazine to remove him from the team. Dawson said he had no interest in being connected with pornography or the enticement of an all-expense paid weekend at the Playboy Mansion. Dawson said many of his teammates didn't understand his decision and when they did ask, he used it as an opportunity to share his faith. Dawson's stance encouraged other collegiate stars over the next 10 years to also turn down this team, including quarterback Danny Wuerffel and lineman Ben Hamilton.

1. Describe a time when you showed tremendous courage in the face of opposition or fear. What did you learn through the experience?
2. How can showing courage make a difference to people around you, including your teammates and/or fans?

Throughout history, people have loved seeing bravery and heroism in action. They are virtues not confined to any single generation, race or religion. Courage is one of the foundation stones of the human spirit. To be called a coward is one of the most piercing statements that could ever be uttered about a person. Popular movies such as "Gladiator", "Braveheart", and "Saving Private Ryan" depict men and women who take courageous stands for ideals they believe. Their heroic stories are compelling and gripping.

Courage comes in various forms:

- Military: In times of battle men move in masses and the momentum carries them forward. Excitement thrills the nerves and heats the blood. The courage of war is often spectacular and appealing to the eye, as the courageous scoff at danger and mock death.

- Physical/Instinct: This type of courage is an indifference to danger, with a strong desire to carry out duties even if fear is involved. For example, my eight year old daughter didn't even blink an eye recently when she entered a neighbor's home after dark to feed the animals while they were out of town.
- Opportunistic: This is born out of a feverish moment, drawn out by some type of overwhelming disaster. Firemen, policemen, rescue crew workers and even normal, everyday people accomplishing daring feats in the face of adversity.

Jefferson states, "In Jesus of Nazareth we find bravery at its best, courage at its loftiest, and heroism at its climax." Jesus' courage was different than military, physical or opportunistic situations. His was for a higher and nobler purpose. He was about courage of the mind and heroism of the heart. He deliberately counted the cost and willingly paid the price for all mankind on the cross. Unlike a military hero, Jesus marched alone. He manifested his courage hour by hour along the dusty road when there was nothing to heat the blood or stir the mind.

In which stories would you identify Jesus as a courageous hero? Was it when he cleansed the temple by driving out the cattle and overturning the tables of the money changers? Was it when he spoke up against the Scribes and Pharisees? Was it in the Garden of Gethsemane when his accusers arrested him? Was it when he struggled while walking up Golgotha? Jefferson says, "All of these images are picturesque and thrilling, but these aren't the best pictures of Jesus' courage."

An early example of his courage was when he announced his mission to the men and women who had known him from childhood—he calmly preached and lived out the truth to his family members. One of the most compelling pictures of Jesus' courage is found in John 6:22-67 when he began speaking to thousands of people in the streets of Capernaum shortly after feeding them in the desert beyond the Sea of Galilee. At the beginning of his address, they were enthusiastic, but as he spoke the crowds dwindled. Eventually only his twelve disciples were left. Jesus asked them, "Will you go away also?" To compare this to modern day life, Jefferson summarized the feelings of most preachers and teachers by saying, "…they find joy in the ears and hearts of those who hear. To hold them, to teach them, to inspire them—this is indeed glorious. But to teach the truth and have the congregation become smaller shows tremendous courage."

1. What is a favorite movie of yours featuring acts of courage? Share one of the compelling scenes of this movie with the rest of the group.
2. Look at the three forms of courage as noted above. Which one of these would be the most difficult one for you to show and why? Which one would be the easiest and why?

Jesus surrendered the positive opinion which many had formed of him when he began his public ministry. When he first appeared the air was filled with excitement. People looked upon him as the promised Messiah. Men and women blazed with enthusiasm. But they had certain ideals, and Jesus couldn't conform to them. Jesus refused to carry out their ideas which contradicted God's plan. He refused to ride the easy road of popularity. It takes tremendous courage to lay aside one's reputation and forego the applause. He was reverent and sensitive, but there were certain things he had to say and do to stay true to God's purpose and will. He spoke the truth even if it meant he would be called a blasphemer, a lunatic and a traitor. How many of us would possess the courage to do the same?

Ironically, that wasn't the climax of Jesus' courage. He withstood his enemies, but the most difficult challenge was having the courage to withstand the pressures of his friends. Peter, James, John and Judas all pressed Jesus with reasonable requests, and yet he stood courageously against their influence and desires.

The Gospels are filled with examples of Jesus' courage. He set his face intently toward Jerusalem, where he knew the soldiers were going to scourge him, spit upon him and kill him. His friends tried to persuade him not go to Jerusalem. But he kept on steadily, knowing that at Jerusalem he would give his life as ransom for many. Jesus' courage never became audacious or reckless. He bore the burden and endured the cross until his work was completed. He was so courageous that he dared to be silent. As a sheep before his shearers, he didn't open his mouth. When he stood before Pilate, he was so erect that Pilate feared him. And when they finally nailed him to the cross he uttered, "Father, forgive them, for they know not what they do."

There are numerous examples of men and women who have been engaged in reformation, being misrepresented and abused, who have quit saying, "I'm tired, or I'm sick, or I'm giving up." Only cowards surrender. Jesus never turned back...even at the cross. He trampled down all the things of this world, placing them beneath his feet. By doing so he demonstrated that we are to set aside all personal ambitions and aspirations, dying to self and being re-born. Everything that is seemingly valuable and worthwhile is secondary to being in a right relationship with God.

How does the courage of Jesus apply to us today? I believe that the type of courage Jesus demonstrated needs to occur within ourselves, in our families, in our work situations, in our churches, on our teams and in our communities. Commonly we find ourselves in compromising situations which challenge our personal ethics. We know what is right and wrong based on the principles outlined in God's Word, yet the pressures of this world often cause us to make foolish and incorrect decisions, demonstrating our lack of courage. At times our desire to be politically correct violates truth. We don't speak the truth because we fear loss of our job, loss of a relationship or loss of our reputation.

It is time for Christians to be courageous. We need to be morally strong in our leadership. We need to be unwavering in our pursuit of excellence. We need to speak the truth in love. We need to be live out Biblical principles. We need to be godly examples to a waiting and watching world. In order to live courageously, we must look to Jesus Christ—the author and perfecter of our faith.

1. How did your view of courage change as you pondered the courage of Jesus? In which situation did Jesus show the most courage? Why?

2. What would be the impact in your world (personally, family, work place, community, team and church) if you demonstrated the same type of courage that Jesus did?

3. Read Galatians 6:9-10. Think about a time when you were weary of doing good. How did you handle the situation?

This week, write out and memorize Joshua 1:9

FIRMNESS

FIRMNESS: Not soft or yielding when pressed; securely fixed in place; steady; not shaking or trembling

In the last high school game of Nate Haasis' career, a late 37-yard touchdown pass was completed with the opponents making no effort to stop the catch. The throw gave Haasis a conference record of 5,006 yards for his career. After the game, both coaches acknowledged arranging the deal during a time out. The following day, Haasis asked league officials to erase his record-setting pass because his coach had made a deal with the opposing team. In his letter to the president of the conference, Haasis asked that the pass be stricken from the record books. "While I admittedly would like to have passed the record, as I think most high school quarterbacks would, I am requesting that the Central State Eight not include this pass in the record books," Haasis wrote. Haasis said the yardage he passed for in his career required a lot of cooperation and hard work from his teammates. He did not wish to diminish the accomplishments that had been made in the last three years.

1. Share a time when you had to stand up for your convictions or beliefs, going against popular opinion or peer pressure. What resulted from your stance?
2. Comment on the Hassis' story on what you would have done from the perspective of the two coaches, league officials and Nate Haasis.

I once worked with a man who was one of the most charming and brilliant men you could ever meet, but his major flaw was wishy-washy behavior. The voices of this world bombarded him at every turn with subtle lies. He waffled in making decisions. He had difficulty saying "yes" to the best because he couldn't say "no" to anything. His internal battles centered around the old adage, "If you don't stand for something, you'll fall for anything." Bottom line—this man struggled with the character quality of firmness.

What does it mean to be a person who is firm? Firmness can be defined as "exerting a tenacity of will with strength and resolve--a willingness to run counter to the traditions and fashions of the world." I believe a man or woman of God should not only be gentle and kind, but underneath the soft velvet must lie a resolve as hard as steel. It takes nerves and guts to resist negative peer pressure. Listen to the warning God gives in 1 Corinthians 15:33, "Do not be deceived, 'Bad company corrupts good morals.'" The Living Bible puts it this way, "Don't be fooled by those who say such things. If you listen to them you will start acting like them." We need to build a will strong enough to resist and control forces that corrupt good morals.

It takes strong character to run counter to the traditions and fashions of the world. To a certain degree we are molded by society. We adapt to the ideas and habits of our peers--many of which can bring us to ruin. We are easily impressed by those who have influence in our personal and professional lives. Even the strongest and most independent people often bow down before the standards against which their conscience revolts and submit to customs against which the heart protests.

Business people, students and even pastors are all susceptible to yielding to the crowds or the influence of dominating minds. Typically people don't want to stand out, especially when it relates to something that is an unpopular opinion. We want to blend into the masses, staying out of the spotlight. The majority of us are not strong enough to be ourselves. We become echoes of our co-workers, neighbors and friends walking in paths marked out by others. So how do we strengthen our resolve and stand firm in our convictions?

Once again, I believe the answer we seek can be found in the life of Jesus Christ. Jesus was never dominated by enemies or friends. He successfully resisted all negative influences and he did it in a loving, tender way, standing firm in his convictions without being obnoxious.

1. How does peer pressure affect you? In what ways is peer pressure like "monkey see, monkey do?"

2. Think of someone you know who is firm but not obnoxious. How is his firmness lived out in a real and authentic way?

Consider some of the many ideas about the role of the Messiah:

- The Messiah was to be a wonder worker, and the manifestations of his power were to be spectacular and overwhelming. People were drawn to Jesus and his miracle powers, and he became well known all over the country.
- The Messiah was to trample opposing forces under his feet and make Israel the center of the world. Jesus heard their cries clamoring for a king who would rise to supremacy over the wrecked empire of Caesar. The nation was ripe for revolution. A word from his mouth would, like a spark, have kindled a mighty fire.
- The people pinned huge dreams and expectations on the Messiah. It is dangerous to go against popular expectations. It is cruel to extinguish the fire of a nation's hope. How could Jesus hope to win the attention of the people or direct their lives unless he carried out their wishes? It was a great temptation, so terrific that he told his apostles all about it. He assured them that in this temptation he had wrestled against Satan, but despite repeated assaults he had come out of the conflict victorious.

In spite of these ideas, Jesus resisted their traditions and teachings. The Pharisees, Sadducees and other religious leaders received his verbal wrath. He didn't accept their forms of worship. He ran counter to the religious right and cut across all prejudices. The Samaritans, the prostitutes, the tax collectors were all friends of his. The true worshippers worship Him in spirit and in truth, rather than with superstitions and ritualistic duties.

Jesus firmly resisted all the voices, standing alone in defiance of what the best men were doing and saying. He refused to be manipulated and used. The seductions they offered couldn't swerve Him off His mission. He wouldn't be bought or moved. He stayed on course to Gethsemane and Golgotha though many tried to tempt him in another direction. He didn't budge. Likewise, today a man of strength will not compromise his principles nor jeopardize the ultimate victory by playing into the hands of men whose goal is different.

Jesus never gave up his principles even to please his friends. For example, there was no person so near to Jesus' heart as his dear friend Simon Peter. Peter tried to dissuade him from a certain fate, but the loyal and loving friend succeeded no better than the most hostile Pharisee. Jesus couldn't be moved by friend or foe. It was his Father's business he attended to. "Get thee behind me Satan," he said to the astonished Peter, recognizing in him the same evil spirit he had contended with years before in the desert.

He faced this same conflict in his home with his brothers and even with his mother. How hard it must have been for Jesus to even go beyond his mother's exhortations.

Jefferson stated, "Firm himself, he loved men who couldn't be moved. Unconquerable himself, he entrusted his message to men who would endure and not flinch. It is in this tenacity of will that we find an indispensable element of Christian character. Men are to resist exterior forces and form their life from within. Not to be swayed by current opinion, but by the spirit of the Eternal Father in their heart. They are not to listen to the voice of time, but to live and work for eternity. We like this steadfastness in human beings, and we crave it in God. For God is unchanging and unchangeable."

Jesus never gave up his principles and the focus of his mission. How about you? Are you living a life of firmness?

Today, I challenge you to consider the example of Christ. Ask him to help you in being a person who stands up for Jesus Christ no matter what the opposition. Live out 1 Corinthians 15:58, "Be steadfast, immovable, always abounding in the work of the Lord...."

1. Peter was nicknamed "the rock," yet there were times when he didn't show good firmness. Read Matthew 26:69-75 and discuss why Peter failed in this time of his life. Contrast the life of Christ compared to the life of Peter related to their firmness.
2. Evaluate your firmness on a scale of 1-10 (1-Not Firm; 10-Firm) based on the definition given above. Why did you rate yourself this way?
3. What are the keys to firmness for you (i.e. what do you need to do to be firm)?
4. In what areas of your life do you need to be more firm?

This week, write out and memorize 1 Corinthians 15:58.

GLADNESS

BECOMING HYSTERICALLY HAPPY

GLADNESS: Abounding in joy, jubilation and cheerfulness.

In 1980, the world watched one of the greatest upsets in sports history as the United States beat the heavily favored Russians in a classic hockey match at the Winter Olympics at Lake Placid, NY. The celebration and utter joy captured the entire country. It was one of the most exciting and unexpected victories ever witnessed. I remember exactly where I was at when the announcer screamed, "Do you believe in miracles?" While everyone enjoys winning and the thrill of victory, there is also the agony of defeat. How we respond to the disappointment of losing is often one of the greatest revealers of our true character. I have seen people deal with losing by getting angry, or crying, while others have shown little or no emotion.

1. Share a time when you won an unexpected victory. What were some of the emotions you experienced?
2. Share a time that you experienced a loss when you expected to win. What were some of the emotions you experienced?
3. How do you deal with losing? What have you learned from past victories and defeats?

Recently a friend handed me an artist's depiction of Jesus Christ. Unlike most pictures I have seen in the past where Jesus appears sad, angry, or solemn, this one showed Jesus roaring in laughter with a huge sparkle in his eye. It was a wonderful, refreshing look at one of the great character qualities Jesus modeled.

Jesus is our example of gladness, and because of him Christians should be the happiest people on the planet. Jefferson said, "What a pity it is to live in a world like this and not enjoy living! It is amazing that anyone should live in a universe so glorious, and not feel like shouting! If you are lachrymose (tearful or mournful) and drooping it is because there is something wrong. You are not well in body or in mind, or it may be you are sick in both. You have not yet learned the high art of living, you have not yet come to Jesus."

Jesus was a man abounding in joy. As he teaches you hear his message breathing gladness. He said, "Unless you change and become like little children, you will never enter the kingdom of heaven." What was it in a little child that attracted Jesus? It was the life, energy and laughter of a child which Jesus applauded. Jesus also urged us to not spend time worrying (Matthew 6:25-33). He asks us to not worry about the present, about the necessities of life, about tomorrow and about what we ought to do or say in the midst of great crisis. He says it is not right to worry about tomorrow because God has it all under control. Gladness can be described as feeling contentment and peace inside, knowing God's in charge outside.

Author Paul Sailhammer says, "Joy is that deep settled confidence that God is in control of every area of my life." Tim Hansel believes, "Joy is not a feeling; it is a choice. It is not based upon circumstances; it is based upon attitude. It is free, but it is not cheap. It is the by-product of a growing relationship with Jesus Christ. It is a promise, not a deal. It is available to us when we make ourselves available to Him. It is something that we can receive by invitation and choice. It requires commitment, courage and endurance."

There is no question that the day-to-day grind of life is difficult. In John 16:33 Jesus reminds us that in the world we will experience trouble. There will be tribulation, but we are not merely to endure it but to "be of good cheer" for He has overcome the world.

He exhorted his disciples when persecuted and in encountering all sorts of evil to "rejoice and be exceedingly glad." The original Greek says it this way, "Rejoice and leap for joy." In other words, when everything is at its worst, you should have a happiness which leaps. He reminds us in Matthew 11:28, 30, "Come to me, all you who are weary and burdened, and I will give you rest. For my yoke is easy and my burden is light." Jesus was glad even to the end. Even in the upper room, when death was only a few hours away, he went right on speaking of the joy that was bubbling up in his heart, and he prayed the same joy would abound in the hearts of those who love him. He wanted them to have joy and that their joy might be full.

1. Identify several people whom you would describe as "glad." What do you think causes them to be that way?
2. Discuss the differences between joy and happiness. Is it possible to have joy and not be happy?

3. Describe how your attitude toward disappointment can affect you and others? Describe how choosing gladness can affect you and others?

Jesus even referred to himself as a bridegroom when addressing gladness. There were lots of talks among the Jewish leaders because Jesus never fasted, nor did he teach his disciples it was their duty to fast. A good Jew fasted twice every week. Fasting was prescribed by the great rabbis, including John the Baptist. Jesus was not anti-fasting and in fact he gave guidelines on appropriate fasting in Matthew 6:16-18. One day some people came to Jesus with disgust saying, "Why do your disciples not fast?" Jesus said, "How can the guests of the bridegroom mourn while he is with them? The time will come when the bridegroom will be taken from them; then they will fast." Jesus' reference to himself as the bridegroom is an intriguing word because a wedding celebration is a symbol of joy. If ever a man is happy in this world, it is on his wedding day. Jesus said he and his disciples lived in an atmosphere of wedding joy. Jesus illustrated this point in this same passage (Matthew 9:14-17) by reminding them to not put a new patch on an old garment and not put new wine into old wine skins. He was saying the new life he was advancing could not be lived out in the old ways.

I believe there are two options for every believer--happy and hysterically happy! You choose whether or not you are going to live life through anxiety and worry or with gladness and enthusiasm. It's a daily decision to choose joy.

How do you live out gladness in the midst of disappointments, frustrations and crushed hopes and dreams? I believe it all boils down to having a deep, personal relationship with God. Ephesians 4:23 tells us, "Be renewed in the spirit of your mind." Enthusiasm comes from the Greek word entheos meaning: God in you, or full of God. The power comes from God himself who gives you the wisdom, courage, strategy and faith necessary to deal successfully with the difficulties of life.

Through faith in Christ we can overcome all the world throws at us. But having this relationship doesn't promise a trouble and problem free life. Out of our struggles come many of the areas of growth that build our character. Tim Hansel says, "Pain is inevitable, but misery is optional. We cannot avoid pain, but we can avoid joy. God has given us such immense freedom that He will allow us to be as miserable as we want to be." John McArthur points out, "There is no event or circumstance that can occur in the life of any Christian that should diminish the Christian's joy."

In closing, I urge you to adopt an attitude of enthusiasm and gladness. Emory Ward once remarked, "Enthusiasm, like measles, mumps and the common cold, is highly contagious." Today, renew your commitment to pursue gladness no matter what obstacles or opportunities come your way. How about becoming contagious today?

1. What picture images come to mind when you think of Jesus? Is this an accurate picture based on what you have just read?
2. From your observation, do Christians handle disappointment better than non-Christians? Why or why not? Can you think of any examples?
3. Satan will try to capitalize on every negative circumstance in your life to bring you down—to steal your gladness. We must be forewarned and forearmed. What are some of the keys to keeping a positive attitude in the midst of difficult situations? Identify specific Scriptures to help with this discussion.
4. Living for Christ is the most dynamic, exciting and fulfilling journey you'll ever experience. How could you explain Christian "gladness" to a non-believer?
5. How do you handle anxiety and worry? In what areas can you give God control of your life?

This week, write out and memorize Psalm 100:2

GREATNESS

GREATNESS: Demonstrating an extraordinary capacity for achievement.

Cal Ripken, whose boyhood dream was to be good enough to play in the minor leagues like his dad, shattered the immortal Lou Gehrig's consecutive major league baseball game record of 2,131 games in 1998. Ripken's streak of 2,632 games began in 1982, spanning 17 straight seasons including an amazing streak of 904 games where he played 8,243 consecutive innings. Gehrig, the Iron Horse of the New York Yankees, had held the record since April 30, 1939. Many people believed Gehrig's record would never be surpassed. Now they are saying the same thing about Ripken's new standard.

When discussing "Greatness" one name tops them all when it comes to basketball—Michael Jordan!! In addition to his many awards and accomplishments on the court, Michael was also recognized as the most admired role model among high school students during his playing days, exceeding great politicians, business men and other influential people.

Every athlete is after greatness, but for many, the pursuit is short lived. One petite athlete has been in pursuit for many, many years now. Michelle Kwan won her eighth United States ice skating title in January 2004. She has been in pursuit of greatness for more than 13 years and doesn't appear to be stopping any time soon. Her next goal is the Olympic games in 2006.

1. Which individuals do you consider great? Identify their accomplishments and honors. How did they impact your life or the world?
2. Compare your answers to Jesus Christ. How does the greatness of Christ look in comparison?

Many of us aspire to be great, both personally and professionally. I know I have desired to be great; as a child I longed to be a famous athlete, and now as a father and minister I want my parenting and ministry to be great. Each of us can call to mind at least a few individuals whom we consider great. Defining greatness, however, becomes a bit tricky. What is it, exactly, that constitutes greatness?

When you scrutinize individuals from history widely acclaimed and revered as immortal, there are various gifts and graces, but no two are identical...none. Yet how are they alike? Is there a similar characteristic among them? I believe the quality common to all of them is an extraordinary capacity for achievement. They each accomplished significant and enduring things, so the world was not the same after they had gotten done with it. Jefferson states, "They carved statues or painted pictures or led armies or ruled states or composed music or framed laws or wrote poems or made discoveries or inventions which enriched the lives and homes of men. They achieved something worthwhile. They made a mark on the mind of the world."

These mortals and their achievements inspire and motivate us, but if we seek to truly define greatness at its core, one man stands alone: Jesus Christ. Oddly, by worldly or tangible standards of greatness, Jesus might not measure up. He never wore a crown or held a scepter or threw on a purple robe. He never held an office in a church or state. He did absolutely nothing in art, literature, science, philosophy, invention, statesmanship, or war. However, not only is he counted great, but he is so great there is no one comparable to him. Jefferson said, "When great men enter the room we should rise to meet them, but if Christ was to come into the room, we should all fall to our knees. His greatness is greater than that of all the others, and it is also different. While others are great at their skills, Jesus was a great man. His greatness lies in the realm of personality, in the kingdom of character and in the greatness of his soul."

Insight is one trait of greatness. Only great men see deep into things. Jesus' insight made him formidable to the men who tried to trip and trap him with their questions. Again and again they tried, but they never succeeded. He was clever, quick, and possessed a transcendent personality. His greatness is illustrated in his relationship with the disciples. Though strong and able, they were a sorry sight in his presence. They were pitiful and thick headed. They weren't able to grasp the simplest teachings. Their tempers and personal ambitions made them even worse. They were petty, envious and selfish, arguing among themselves as to which one of them should hold the highest place in heaven.

Can anyone compare to Jesus? Great men have come and gone, but His soul is unique, incomparable, unapproachable, and unending. Jesus' greatness is revealed by the length, width and depth of his achievements. Similarly, human greatness is also measured by the effect it produces. Men cannot be judged by stature or physical characteristics alone; greatness doesn't lie merely in words or even in actions. The total effect of a man's life in both public and private determine the level of greatness he achieves. Typically, those closest to a great man rarely share the level of respect afforded him by the public because they see his day in and day out humanness. Not so with Jesus.

1. What makes a person great? Is it appropriate to pursue greatness?
2. Do you ever get tired of trying to be great and not seeing results?
3. How does one know when he has arrived at greatness?

The effect Jesus had on others was significant, so significant that his apostles were influenced beyond their own personalities. One man, Thomas, was methodical and cool. He wasn't carried away by emotions. But one day he exclaimed, "Let us go and die with him." Thomas was so drawn to him he was ready to die for him and so were the other apostles. In the last hours, Peter announced he was ready to go with Jesus to prison and to death yet minutes later his courage oozed out. Peter's cowardice was only temporary, and years later he fulfilled his declaration to Jesus. Ultimately all the apostles, except for John, were martyrs for him.

To influence others to the point where they are willing to give up their lives for someone else or a cause is extraordinary. This is the climax of power. Jesus changed men. He changed their habits, opinions, ambitions, tempers, dispositions and natures. He changed their hearts. The disciples were never the same after giving themselves up to him. This is greatness indeed.

The things Jesus did in Palestine he has been doing ever since. Wherever his story is told, thoughts and feelings change. He has transformed ideals and institutions. When he speaks, people overflow with emotion. This one man changed the entire course of human history.

Jesus is full of grace and truth. His dimensions are complete—his virtues are in fullest bloom; his eyes look to eternity; his sympathy covers all of humanity; his purpose spans all lands and ages; and his kingdom is universal, having no end. He pushes every good trait of human character to its outermost limit. His forgiveness is unbounded, his generosity untiring, his patience inexhaustible, his mercy immeasurable, his courage limitless, his wisdom unfathomable, and his kindness and love infinite. It is impossible to go beyond him. We can never outgrow him, and we will always need him.

His name is above all names. He exerts power with a phenomenal capacity. He is the Son of God. He is victorious, and we are told that one day every knee will bow and every tongue will confess that he is King indeed.

What makes a person great? Is it appropriate to pursue greatness? How does one know when he has arrived at the moment of greatness? At times my desire for greatness has been for my own personal gain and at other times, I've wanted to pursue greatness to glorify God. Like James and John in Matthew 20:20-25, I have frequently sought greatness to promote myself and my agenda. Jesus reminds me that greatness is found in becoming teachable like a little child (Matthew 18:1-5); in becoming a servant (Matthew 20:26-28); and in becoming obedient to his call on my life (Philippians 2:6-11). Today, acknowledge his greatness in a way you have never done before. Remove pride, acknowledge weakness and give your life to the greatest man of all--Jesus!!

1. Read these verses – Matthew 18:1-5; Matthew 20:20-28 and Philippians 2:6-11 – and discuss the following:
    a. What does Jesus tell us about greatness?
    b. Why does Jesus use a little child to describe greatness?
    c. How did Jesus Christ become great?
2. Jesus challenges us to serve if we want to attain greatness. How do servants become great? How have you seen this occur?
3. How has Jesus Christ changed you? How has he changed the people around you?
4. What are you in pursuit of today: athletic glory or God's glory? Today, how can you start to pursue God's greatness?

This week, write out and memorize Matthew 20:26-28.

HOLINESS

BE HOLY FOR I AM HOLY

HOLINESS: Having no blemish or stain; being whole with no trace of regret or remorse.

During the 1970's the Baltimore Orioles employed a devout outfielder named Pat Kelly, who presided at clubhouse chapel services that seemed eccentric at the time. Until that time, God wasn't invited into the locker room. Today, prior to virtually every professional and collegiate game and many high school games, volunteer chapel leaders share God's Word with players and coaches. These chapel services are a big part of the pregame routine for many of the participants. With the NBA, chapel services are held prior to every game with attendees from both teams. In the NFL and Major League Baseball, chapel services are on Sundays. Many of the players have shared how valuable this time is in keeping their priorities in focus.

1. Did you realize many teams employ a volunteer chaplain to help conduct devotional and worship services for teams prior to ball games? What do you think of this?
2. Have you ever been part of a sports chapel? If so, share your personal experience.

Chapel is now a big part of a player's pregame routine before going on the field. While attendance is voluntary, those who participate are often perceived by their teammates as "holy" men. In reality, those who attend probably are more aware of their unholy thoughts and lifestyle than those who don't attend.

Have you ever had someone refer to you as "holy"? One time a person called me a "holy man" and I mumbled in response, "You have no idea of how unholy I really am." Underneath the outward appearance is my soul which hides the secrets of my heart. When it comes to holiness, I know what I am and the horrible things I am capable of doing and saying. It is not a pretty picture, especially when I compare myself to the King of Kings and Lord of Lords, Jesus Christ. I know I am a sinner, saved only by the grace of God.

According to Jefferson, "Only Jesus Christ is great enough to hold the title of 'holiness.'" By definition, "holiness" means wholeness and full-orbed perfection. A holy man is a man without a fleck or flaw, a character without a blemish or stain. Jesus certainly qualifies as holy. However, 1 Peter 1:16 challenges us, "Be holy, because I am holy." How do we do this? Let's first take a look at Jesus.

Scripture tells us Jesus was without sin. Not one single thought was stained. Every motive, even the deepest thought, was in line with the will of God. His words and actions were absolutely right in God's sight, including when he drove the merchants out of the temple and when he cursed the fig tree.

There is nothing in Jesus' consciousness which indicates he was guilty of any sin. There is no trace anywhere of regret or remorse. Throughout the Gospels, he is seen as serene, jubilant, confident and free. Sin has a way of casting a dark shadow over our conscience, but there is nothing to indicate this was the case with Jesus. Jefferson says, "Virtually everyone agrees that Jesus was a good man, exceedingly good and beyond this, extraordinarily good. Many will admit that he was the best man that ever lived. But if you admit this, you have to go a great deal farther. For in the same proportion as his spiritual sense is keen to sin, the consciousness of the sin becomes disturbing and appalling. The higher a man rises in spiritual attainment, the more he is knowledgeable of his sin."

Isaiah, Job, John, Paul, Peter--each of them was aware of the sin that resided within his heart. Every human being who has taken a good hard look at his humanness cries out like the Psalmist, "Have mercy upon me, O God...blot out my transgressions...wash away all my iniquity and cleanse me from my sin...for my sin is always before me" (Psalm 51:1-3). Peter was a godly man, a tireless worker for the church, but when it came time to die he requested he be crucified upside down because he felt unworthy to die as Jesus died because of his sin. Paul, too, was distraught by his earlier life recognizing his sin of persecuting believers. He identified himself as the "chief of all sinners." Jesus was different than these men because he was holy. There was never any need for him to be ashamed of his human condition because he was without sin.

1. What do you think of when you hear the word "holy"? Do you see yourself as a holy person?
2. Read Leviticus 11:44-45 and 1 Peter 1:13-16. Why does God call us to live a holy life?
3. Jesus was without sin. Why is holiness a crucial character quality for Jesus? Why is our pursuit of holiness important as well?

The extraordinary effect Jesus had on others confirms his holiness. John the Baptist was initially reluctant to baptize him because Jesus was without sin. Jesus' reply to him wasn't, "I am a sinner, therefore I must be baptized." No, he says, "It is proper for us to do this to fulfill all righteousness." In 1 John 3:5 we read, "He appeared so that he might take away our sins. And in him is no sin." Peter was with him day and night and in 1 Peter 2:22 he says, "He committed no sin, and no deceit was found in his mouth." These men were with Jesus. They ate and drank with him, seeing him in all conditions and in various circumstances. They saw him hungry, angry, stern, surprised, disappointed, amazed, yet they testified he committed no sin. In Hebrews 4, we are told Jesus was tempted in all ways as we are, yet he was without sin.

The only one who can claim perfection is Jesus Christ. His life was full of suffering and persecution; it ended in a horrible death, yet His soul was radiantly holy. Nothing creates gloom in this world like sin. Even the vilest of sinners knows the war raging deep down in his soul when sin is unchecked. Literally, sin makes his spirit droop and no relief is found in his conscious.

Jesus' sinlessness explains his joyfulness. We are drawn to him because of his holiness. His sinlessness gives the Christian church its power. There is only one perfect possession in the church, and it is Jesus Christ. The church is far from perfect but Jesus of Nazareth, the head of the church, is stainless and triumphant. We worship him as God because he is holy and perfect.

Jesus, the Lamb of God, died for us that we might become holy. Colossians 1:22 says, "He has now reconciled (you) in his body of flesh by his death, in order to present you holy and blameless and above reproach before him." The sinless Christ never turns away from us, no matter how sinful we are. He says, "Come unto me." He is willing to wash away the stains. He is the Lamb of God that takes away the sin of the world, and thus he chooses to make us holy.

Christians in the early church are often referred to as saints. The word saint conjures up images of a super-righteous person, a person of extraordinary piety and spiritual power. Yet, in the New Testament all the people of God are referred to as saints. The word simply means "holy one." It may seem odd for the term to be used of believers who were struggling with all kinds of sin. When you read Paul's epistles, he addresses them as saints and then rebukes them for their foolish and sinful behavior. The saints in Scripture were called saints not because they were already pure but because they were people who were set apart and called to purity.

"Be holy for I am holy." This simple command is for everyone who claims to be a Christian. It is the high calling of God on our lives which enables us to lead organizations, manage people and conduct our daily affairs with integrity and holiness. It is recognizing our need to draw close to Jesus Christ for everything, not putting ourselves in inappropriate situations. The character quality of holiness can only be attained when we are in total alignment with the holy one—Jesus Christ. How aligned are you?

1. Our problem is that we have been called to be holy, and yet we are not holy. How can we reconcile this difference?
2. The Bible calls us "holy ones." We are holy because we have been consecrated to God. We have been set apart. We have been called to a life that is different. How can you live out a life which is holy in the sight of God and man?
3. How can we know if we are making real progress in our quest to be holy?
4. In what ways do you want to grow in holiness in the next year?

This week, write out and memorize 1 Peter 1:16

NARROWNESS

TRAVELING DOWN THE NARROW PATH

NARROWNESS: Staying within established boundaries and limits.

Coach Tom Osborne had just finished warning his team during the halftime break to keep their mouths shut and not respond to the comments made by the other team. As the 1995 Huskers took the field against Miami in the national championship game, assistant coach Ron Brown credited much of their second half success to self-discipline and a willingness to heed Coach Osborne's advice. "We knew as coaches that the 1995 Hurricane team was likely to push us into a trash-talking game. Coach Osborne knew we were better conditioned, so if we could keep from responding to their verbal taunts, we could win the game," Brown said. Nebraska resisted the temptation to respond to the trash-talking Warren Sapp and his teammates during the second half. This focused attitude helped lead the Cornhuskers to a victory that would become Coach Osborne's first national championship.

1. Share a time when you maintained focus in the midst of a chaotic situation. What ultimately resulted?
2. Define "narrowness" in the context of your athletics or work.

What's the difference between a river and a swamp? A river only becomes a river by the assistance of its banks. So, rivers have banks and swamps do not. A river becomes mightier and more majestic when the mountains press against it. When a river spreads out beyond strong established banks it eventually becomes shallow, muddy and feeble. A river through a narrow channel has depth, strength and significance. When we are pressed against the mountains through sorrows, calamity and new responsibilities, our channel narrows and we experience richness and significance.

I meet many men who tell me that they are buried in the chaos of life. They are overwhelmed juggling many different responsibilities. Many have told me that they are trying to "simplify" their lives by saying "no" to the good things in order to say "yes" to the best. Dan

Erickson has often said, "I fear at succeeding at something that doesn't matter." Jefferson, "The most galling of all experiences is the failure to do that which is the most worthwhile."

Narrowness is often thought of as a negative word because many view it as being one-sided rather than open-minded. Instead, it refers to the boundaries established for living. If you are looking for an example of narrowness consider Jesus Christ's:

- Geography: Jesus lived his life in Palestine--a little country no larger than Connecticut. A simple, rural community. He could've traveled to Rome or Athens like other great teachers, but he stayed and poured out his life on the villages of Judea.
- Obscurity: For his first 30 years he remained in a dingy carpenter's shop and except for one incident at 12 years old, we know very little about Him.
- Focus: Jesus could have done a thousand good things; but he left 999 unattempted tasks and confined Himself to the one thing that His heavenly Father had given Him to do. In Luke 13:24 a man asked him, "Make my brother divide the inheritance with me!!" It was a noble request but Jesus' reply was: "No....that lies outside my duties." Had he wandered around speaking parables to everyone and healing every need, he might have had more ears but he would have molded fewer hearts. Because he focused on a few people, he became increasingly influential.
- Ministry: While others, including the disciples, wanted him to do more to make an impression on people, he refused to listen to them because it wasn't his time. Later when He knew it was time to go, the same disciples tried to divert Him from going to Jerusalem. Jesus stayed on track to His goal despite the peer pressure.

Jefferson said, "No man can do everything, no man should attempt everything." Jesus was on a mission and He didn't waste a single minute. When he spoke he often said, "I must, I must, I must." There were broad roads on his right and left, and along these roads thousands of his countrymen were traveling, but he couldn't go with them. When he speaks to people about the narrow road and the broad road, He's speaking out of His own experiences. He urges people to choose the narrow one rather than the broad one, and He only says, "Follow me."

1. Do you need to simplify your life? What areas of your life are chaotic and out of control?
2. What are the personal benefits of being a narrow minded person?
3. Reflect and respond to the Erickson and Jefferson quotes. What are these men trying to tell us about narrowness?

Jesus made no compromises. He wouldn't bend. He maintained an unflinching persistency to the things which He knew were true and good. Jesus looked through the exterior of men's hearts, and He judged them with fearlessness. He didn't minimize the heinousness of sin by treating men alike. He was narrow in His judgments. He refused to let bad men feel they were good. He pursued the narrow way.

Many people in their teens and beyond struggle with what they're going to do. There are so many possibilities and ambitions and much to explore and do. Only when we pick out God's plan do we really begin living and experience joy. Jesus stayed focused on the mission, and he hit the same nail on the head until it was driven in completely.

Here's the principle: An artist becomes "fine" when he maintains narrowness to certain limitations, not becoming careless. A musician has no leeway. He can't be a little sharp or flat—he must be precise and exact. A poet has to stay within a certain rhythm. Musicians, artists and poets all have to be accurate, precise and exact or their art lacks. But living is even more intense than the arts. Jefferson stated, "One cannot think anything he pleases, or feel as he wants to, or act as he is inclined. He must walk the narrow path."

Jesus came to do one thing—to perform the work the Father gave Him to do. At the end, he simply said, "It is finished." Jesus walked the narrow path because of His great love for us, in order that we might have life and have it abundantly.

How does narrowness relate to being "open?" Should we confine ourselves to a single religion or to one particular belief? Should the windows and doors of our minds be kept open to all kinds of wacky thoughts and beliefs? Jesus had no sympathy for this kind of openness. He knew certain thoughts about God were true while others were false; some things were correct and other things had errors; certain duties were uplifting and others were degrading. Jesus clung to truth and he combated the false. He held on to clear-cut positions and he expressed them with vigor and emphasis.

Jesus had eyes that looked through the exterior of men's hearts, and he judged them with a fearlessness which made them melt. Some of the most influential men of Jerusalem he called "fools, blind men, serpents and vipers." He didn't minimize sin by treating certain people differently. He considered all men alike, calling things the way he saw them. He refused to let bad men feel that they were good.

Jesus knew the narrow path would lead to life while the broad road led to death. Jesus was confident of the call on his life which resulted in his joy. We often blunder because we give to many causes, and the result is a lack of joy because we are spread too thin. We can't contribute to every good cause that comes our way.

Jesus calls men everywhere to become his followers. He is rigorous in his commands and demands. He says, "Come unto me and follow me and abide in me." He limited himself and emptied himself of his glory and walked the narrow path so we might have life to the fullest. Consider the road you are traveling. Is it the narrow path or the broad road?

1. Read Matthew 7:13-14. What are these verses telling us about "narrowness?"
2. Would you describe yourself as a "narrow" person? How do you handle life when boundaries, limits or guidelines are established?
3. Do you feel like you are operating within the boundaries of your passions? How long have you felt this way?
4. When someone is trying to get you to do something you believe is questionable or wrong, what is the best way to say no?
5. How could you benefit by narrowing your focus? What action steps could you take today to reach this goal?

This week, write out and memorize John 10:10.

OPTIMISM

OPTIMISM: Endeavoring to see all the possibilities and capacities of the human heart; confident, hopeful and never doubtful.

Ken Griffey Jr. just wanted to be a normal teen-ager, with an emphasis on normal. However, being the son of an All-Star baseball player, and on a fast track himself to stardom made him anything but normal. At one point he felt the price and the sacrifices were too great. At age 18, he was fed up with the pressure of living and swallowed several hundred aspirin tablets in an attempted suicide. Later, Griffey went public with his story. "Don't ever try to commit suicide," he said. "I am living proof how stupid it is." Athletes often have few outlets for relief because every day they are expected to perform at a high level.

1. When have you felt the most pressure in sports?
2. How did that pressure make you feel? How did it affect your performance?

Tim was one of most enthusiastic men I had ever encountered. Bad weather, cranky people, job deadlines, personal stress....nothing ever seemed to faze him. As a key leader in his organization, he had tremendous responsibilities and potential headaches facing him every day on the job. At home, he juggled multiple roles as daddy to his thee young sons. He was also a talented communicator and a nationally known speaker. It seemed like everyone wanted a piece of Tim. In the face of daily crisis, he had an amazing ability to view every situation as an opportunity to trust God to supply all of his needs and desires. Rather than focusing on the negative, Tim chose to be joyful.

Perhaps you've known people like Tim who are positive in spirit. Unfortunately, people like Tim are rare. We could probably name ten people who are negative, whiny, belligerent, angry and a royal pain in the neck before coming up with one optimistic person.

Optimism is much more than positive thinking. It's an unshakable confidence in God, knowing He is working out His sovereign plan. Optimism is a by-product of contentment. We can be optimistic when we know who we are and whose we are.

Jefferson tells us that the world is filled with superficial optimists and shallow, short sighted pessimists. He states, "The superficial optimists are happy go lucky people who are out of touch. Their irrational behavior comes about because they have a shallow brain and a stupid heart. They insist that everything is okay with the world when obviously it is not. The silly grin on their face offers little in terms of solutions. On the flip side, the shallow, short sighted pessimists have an overpowering negative attitude that totally paralyzes them from making productive contributions. They always see shadows; their ears are ready for discord; their eyes seek out tragedy. They listen to the sighs and sobbing of the world. Festering sores are everywhere throughout society and there is absolutely no hope at all."

Our world is filled with people who live daily in these extremist positions. Opposite of these two extremes stands the Man, Jesus Christ. Though He was God, He came to us in bodily form 2000 years ago. He experienced similar sufferings and temptations just like us, as noted in Hebrews 2:9-18. However, he saw everything with eyes wide open. He saw things others didn't notice. He saw agony in every form. He heard every distress and sigh. He saw every sin and evil, but He remained undaunted. He never lost hope.

The latter part of each Gospel could be considered one of the most depressing accounts ever written because of the dismal story of Christ's rejection and death; yet really, it is a jubilant, exhilarating and glorious section of Scripture. Christ inspires confidence and gives us hope. Jefferson tells us, "We need a man with an open eye, open ear, open heart—a man who sees things as they are. Give us a man who feels the fury of the storm, and is certain of the calm which is to follow."

1. What are some areas of your life where you feel stressed out?
2. Do you consider yourself an optimist or a pessimist? Why?
3. What do you think makes life worth living?
4. If a friend said, "I wish I were dead!" what would you say or do? Do you view suicide as a valid option?

Why was Jesus optimistic? First of all, He had an abiding confidence in God. Jesus never doubted. His vision was unclouded. His trust was absolute. He lived in a society that was disgustingly corrupt. Jesus was mistreated and hated. The government was tyrannical and rotten. The Jewish church was formal, lifeless and hypocritical. The leaders of the land were dead to the movements of God's Spirit. However, even in His darkest hour on the eve of His crucifixion in the Garden of Gethsemane, He believed that God was still totally in charge of His life.

Secondly, along with an unwavering trust in God, He accepted people right where they were. In spite of human sin, vices, and frailties—He saw a soul created in God's image. The examples are plentiful in the Gospels: Simon Peter, Zaccheus, Matthew and the prostitutes are just a few of the people who Jesus challenged to a new life. He believed that men and women who had fallen all the way to the bottom could climb back again with God's touch. Jesus knew that anyone could change and become a brand new creation (2 Corinthians 5:17). God's message of love and forgiveness is available to all.

Despite our imperfections and many weaknesses, Jesus sees beyond the surface, and He has confidence in us. He sees our capabilities and the possibilities. Because of our numerous past failures we say there is no use trying any more, but He forgives us when we repent and He says, "Try again." His patience and mercy are infinite. How does it make you feel to know that God is enthusiastic about you? It's a little overwhelming for me because I know I'm not perfect, nor will I ever attain perfection. Yet I realize that I must not listen to my feelings but instead go to God's Word to find out what he says about me. Here are four reasons why God is optimistic about His people:

- Pedigree: We are perfectly designed and created by God (Psalm 139:13-16)
- Position: We are a child (son and daughter) of the King (John 1:12)
- Process: God isn't finished in completing His work in us (Ephesians 2:10 & Philippians 1:6)
- Potential: The "real" you—that which God is developing—is within you (1 Samuel 16:7)

The Christian is called to face life realistically. Dietrich Bonhoeffer reminds us that a realist doesn't deny the importance of faith and prayer, nor does he become hard and skeptical. He says, "The realist approaches life responsibly and is not prepared to let 'pie in the sky' dreams determine important life responses and responsibilities." A realist looks at life in light of God's grace, action and involvement. A belief in God's infinite patience, mercy and love changes the way you view life and the situations encountered.

The Christian man and woman should be the most optimistic person in his or her organization, team, community and neighborhood. There should be an underlying confidence that allows us to live life to the abundance (John 10:10). The challenge for believers in Christ is to place our confidence not in people, places, titles or things but rather in God and His Word.

Bonhoeffer summarizes it well with these timely words, "We are not nothing. Nor are we God. We have significance, but we are fallen. We are capable of great good as well as horrendous evil. We are frequently contradictory, but we are also capable of consistency and single-mindedness. But none of these things adequately describe who we really are. What does describe us more fully is that we are made in God's image, and are loved by God and enabled by Him to live life in faith, trust, and obedience." These truths from God's Word contradict the world's messages which tell us that we have no value. You are loved!! That's why Jesus died for you.

1. On a scale of 1-10 how would you rate yourself (1-Optimist and 10-Pessimist)? Would the people you are closest to, including family members, friends and co-workers, agree with your rating? Why?

2. Discuss the four bullet points above and read the Scripture verses. How do they make you feel? Why is it difficult to remember these simple truths on a daily basis?

3. The Christian is called to face life realistically. React and respond to Bonhoeffer's quote. Do you face life realistically? Give an example.

4. Read Hebrews 2:9-18. Jesus experienced similar sufferings and temptations just like us. How did Jesus handle the stresses of life?

5. How have you experienced God's infinite patience and mercy? How has Christ's optimism about you played a crucial role in your journey of faith?

This week, write out and memorize Philippians 1:6.

ORIGINALITY

THERE ARE NO ORDINARY PEOPLE

ORIGINALITY: Creating "new" thinking, ideas and expanding truths from an independent viewpoint.

Jim Abbott, a one-handed major league baseball pitcher, is one of the most remarkable athletes of all time. In spite of his obvious handicap, Abbott dreamed of simply playing baseball because he wanted to be with his friends. He found a way to pitch and catch a ball even when teams tried to take advantage of his disability. On one occasion, a team bunted six times in a row against him. His first collegiate win came when the opponents tried to steal home on a catcher's throw back to the plate. Abbott's greatest game was when he threw a no-hitter at Yankee Stadium. Many of us would consider Jim Abbott's unique physical handicap a challenge, but he viewed his originality as a gift.

1. Describe some of your physical, emotional, mental, social and spiritual qualities that make you unique.
2. What do you spend most of your time thinking and dreaming about?

Have you ever fully comprehended that every snowflake that falls from the sky, every star in the heavens and every individual who has walked this planet is uniquely created in the image of God? Medical science validates God's Word, telling us the DNA of every person is different. There is no one like you. God designed every single detail of your body, including the color of your skin, eyes and hair. As Psalm 139:15 says, "You know me inside and out, you know every bone in my body; You know exactly how I was made, bit by bit, how I was sculpted from nothing into something."

Amazing by itself, our bodily design is only one small part of a much bigger picture. Our natural talents, skills and personality were also crafted by him. Literally, we are 100% original--not an accident or an afterthought. God never does anything accidental and he never makes mistakes. Every man and woman is designed with a purpose in mind.

Author C.S. Lewis remarked, "There are no ordinary people." Dan Erickson, of People Matter Ministries, agrees and has devoted his life to helping people "discover, develop and deploy their fingerprint of potential." According to Dan, "Every person has something unique to offer and contribute to society, but the average person dies and never realizes his full potential." This is primarily true because they haven't answered four key questions about their existence:

1. Who am I? This deals with identity.
2. Whose I am? This addresses value and importance to God.
3. What is my purpose in life? This answers the question of why we were created.
4. What am I destined to become? This reveals our potential impact.

It is important for people to wrestle with these questions and come to realize that God has asked us to respond by faith to his plans and purposes for our lives, embracing our originality, not conforming to worldly standards and expectations. Let's consider Jesus Christ as a prelude to this discussion on "originality."

Was Jesus original? The word "originality" doesn't appear in the New Testament, but not one person of his day ever doubted whether Jesus was original. Jesus' teaching shook Palestine out of its lethargy, striking his contemporaries as novel. No man had ever spoken this way. Was he one of the early prophets reincarnated? They had no easy explanations for his brilliant insights. Jesus was so different than other teachers that he left the Scribes and Pharisees quivering. If he had repeated the old teachings in the old way, he would not have infuriated them. Jefferson commented, "He was too original to be endurable, he advanced too many strange and revolutionary ideas to make it safe for the land to hold him; it was because he made all things new that they nailed him to the cross."

Was Jesus original? It depends on what you mean by originality. If to be original one must coin words never heard before and speak in phrases no other tongue has ever used, then Jesus was not original. He coined no new words, and many of his phrases have the flavor of olden times. Nor did he proclaim that his ideas had never entered the minds of men. All his main ideas of God and the human soul had been proclaimed by men of God before his arrival. Does this surprise you? It shouldn't, because God had been revealing Himself to people all the way back to creation. All that Jesus taught had been anticipated, and his coming fulfilled the words that the prophets had spoken. He didn't come to destroy the old ideas or old truths but to fulfill each of them. God was now going to speak his full message through his Son.

1. The Bible says you are "fearfully and wonderfully made" (Psalm 139:14). Is it hard for you to think of yourself like this? Why?
2. Go back and answer the four questions posed by Dan Erickson above.
3. Answer the four questions posed by Dan Erickson in the context of how Jesus Christ would answer them.

Jesus' originality came in the way he emphasized his words. He would read a familiar passage in the book of Isaiah, but he gave it an emphasis which had never been heard. For example, he made religion new by emphasizing mercy instead of sacrifice. The result was that it burst upon the people with the force of fresh revelation. People had been reading the Scriptures, but they didn't fully understand it--Jesus did.

Jesus also spoke with a deep assurance, certainty and authority that had never been heard before. He didn't hesitate or speculate, and he never wavered. He was always positive, certain and infallible. His purpose in life was very clear when he said, "I have come to do the will of my Father."

This confidence and the emphasis of his words produced originality. Even the Roman soldiers admitted they had never before seen a man like this. He possessed the faculties common among men, but his combined strength of passion, articulation and wisdom was unique. Jesus was complete and full in his presence. He was different than any other man who had ever lived. He claimed to be the light of the world, the bread of life, the water of life, the only good shepherd, the way, the truth, the life, the only mediator between God and man, the only one knowing deity completely and the only Savior capable of saving the world from its sins. This is unique and in every sense original.

Jefferson noted, "John, who knew Jesus best, heard him say, 'Behold I make all things new.' He could say this because he was new himself. Only Jesus can make something new. He gives us a changed attitude toward life, teaches us how to shift emphasis from unimportant to important words, by showing us the insignificance of "show" compared to love from a pure heart, by taking away our fears, by teaching us about faith and hope, and by bringing us into the light. Jesus did it to Paul. Paul was a scholar and familiar with the key teachings, but these wonderful writings didn't reach the core of Paul's heart until he met Jesus, and everything became new. From that day on the road to Damascus until he died, Paul urged men to cast off the old man and put on the new."

Are you struggling with your identity and your purpose in life? Have the voices of this world robbed you of your originality? What can be done? Go to Jesus and give yourself afresh to him. Sink your life deeper into his and catch his ways of seeing things and serving God. Take his stance, assume his attitude, catch his emphasis, drink in his confident voice, and he will do for you just as he did to Saul of Tarsus. He will make all things new, giving you hope.

Jesus Christ simplifies and transforms all life because he is the Master and Savior. Paul reminds us, "If any man is in Christ, he is a new creature...old things are passed away, behold all things are new." Walk in his newness today as you celebrate your originality.

1. How can you embrace and celebrate your originality?
2. Read the following verses and respond to each one of these statements:
   • God loves you and He's pleased with you because he made you individually (Matthew 3:16-17).
   • God desires an intimate relationship with you—not religion, just a relationship
   (Romans 5:9-11; 8:14-17).
   • God desires to transform you into the image of his Son
   (Romans 8:28-29).
   • God desires to give you his purpose for your life (Philippians 3:13-14).
   • God desires to channel your passion into His purpose
   (Matthew 6:19-21).
3. What did you learn about yourself during this lesson?

This week, write out and memorize Romans 8:28.

POISE

MAINTAINING BALANCE IN ALL SITUATIONS

POISE: Being totally balanced in mind, body and spirit.

The newspaper headlines read, "Vikes surprisingly rely on Culpepper's poise." During the 2000 NFL football season, the Minnesota Vikings got off to a surprising 5-0 start with a young, untested quarterback. Coach Dennis Green was confident Dante Culpepper was good enough to fit into a system that seemed to tolerate quarterbacks more than it needs them. Somebody had to get the ball to Randy Moss, Cris Carter and Robert Smith, and it never seemed to matter whether it was Brad Johnson, Randall Cunningham or Jeff George. Yet, in their victory over Tampa Bay and its tough defense, the Vikings offense was shaky and inconsistent and needed the benefit of two Tampa fumbles. But when it came time for big plays, it was Culpepper hitting two touchdown passes and running for a touchdown. Culpepper's poise in the midst of the game was cited as the key ingredient to his team's victory.

1. Define poise in your own words. How do you show poise in your life?
2. Share an experience where you have seen poise make a winning difference on the job or during a game.

Talk about "poise" comes up often in big time sporting events. After a key win, coaches will comment on how their team maintained poise in the midst of a demanding situation. Poise is a key character quality because it reveals whether or not you are balanced.

Have you ever tried to balance a cane or a long stick on the tip of your finger? Initially I struggled to keep it there for longer than a few seconds, but with practice I can now hold it absolutely still for long periods of time. My ability to balance this cane is a result of the counteraction of two or more opposing forces.

The dictionary defines poise as "a state of balance or equilibrium; dignified and composed in all situations." Rarely do we find a person who is well balanced and poised. Jefferson said, "The average man is one-sided, unsymmetrical and unevenly developed." Typically our bodies aren't perfect. One arm, leg or ear may be slightly larger or different than the other one and in some extremes we call this difference a disability. While it is rare to be perfectly symmetrical in our bodies, it is rarer to find a person who has a balanced mind and spirit.

Jefferson reminds us, "Every virtue pushed beyond its appointed limit becomes a vice, and every grace when overdeveloped becomes a defect or disfiguration." For example, it's great to be enthusiastic but to be overly enthusiastic is fanaticism. Having emotion is fine but too much emotion leads to hysterics. It's wonderful to be imaginative but being exceedingly imaginative is flighty. We all need to be practical and level headed but it can also lead to dullness. Courage is a great quality but excessive courageousness can also tend to be reckless. Being original and unique is wonderful but it could classify you as an eccentric. Even our religious behavior can sometimes slip into superstition.

When we look at other people it is easy for us to remark, "Oh, if he did not have so much of that!" or "If she only had a little more of this." What we are saying in those remarks is we see someone out of balance.

When we look at Jesus we see a man who was totally balanced without any flaw in his mind and spirit. He was well rounded and complete. Jefferson states, "He had in him all the virtues, and not one of them was overgrown. He exhibited all the graces, and every one of them was in perfect bloom. He stands in history as the one man beautiful, symmetrical and absolutely perfect."

In every person there is either something lacking or too much of something, which creates a character flaw. But Jesus was without flaw—He never lacked nor did he go to extremes. He had unrivaled poise in conduct. He lived His life in a whirlwind, constantly being mobbed by people who wanted something from Him, yet He never wavered. He was never entrapped or never tripped up. His enemies never caught Him and their questions never incriminated Him. He escaped it all.

1. Every positive character quality can become detrimental when it goes to an extreme. Using the following words as a starter discuss the extremes sharing the positives and negatives

associated with each: patience, love, faith, trust, hope—add other character words to this discussion as they come to mind.

2. What are the keys to Jesus' poise? NOTE: We'll get some insight into this question in the section below.

As a twelve year old boy, his poise emerged. The old men were astonished at his answers. When he began his public ministry, seductive voices tried to whisper in his ear trying to promote their own agenda. Satan tried to lure him with enticing propositions, but he responded by quoting Scripture. Men tried to convict him of breaking the Sabbath laws, but he instantly proved from Scripture and from reason that what he did was right. When Peter protested his going to Jerusalem where he would be killed, Jesus said, "Get thee behind me, Satan." Jefferson said, "He had heard that voice before. He recognized it even on the lips of his friend. It is one of the devil's last resources to speak through the mouth of a friend. Such a trick cannot deceive Jesus."

On the last Tuesday of his life, the Pharisees put together a scheme to put him in prison. They asked, "Is it right for us to pay taxes to Caesar or not?" It was a trick question. If he said "yes" then he would be hated by every patriotic Jew who believed it was not right to pay Jewish money into a Gentile treasury. If he answered "no" then he proved himself to be a traitor to Rome, and the Roman officials could immediately pounce upon him. How did he answer their question? Holding the money in his hands he said, "Give to Caesar what is Caesar's, and to God what is God's." It was the perfect answer, stopping the Pharisees right in their tracks.

He was also an undisputed conqueror. His poise disconcerted and dumbfounded the high priests, the Pharisees and even Pilate. Not one of Jesus' enemies was able to catch him in His speech, and when they finally convicted Him they did it with a trumped up lie. Jesus was so firmly poised that under the pressure of the most venomous attack ever hurled against a man, He stood erect, unmoved and unmovable. Today, because He was so well balanced and poised, people look to Him for inspiration. There is a grace about Him which does not fade. He has no blemish.

One of the greatest resources I've used in my pursuit of poise comes from Charles Hummel's book, *Tyranny of the Urgent.* Mr. Hummel tells us how Jesus Christ managed and controlled His time while He was on earth. The key to Christ's success was that He received His daily instructions in quiet moments with the Father. Nothing came in the way of His intimate time with God. If Jesus needed this time with God, how much more do you and I need to seek it out?

My ability to live life filled with poise is directly tied to my time alone with God. I'm much better prepared to handle the pressures and stresses of my day if I spend time alone with God early each morning. Psalm 5:1-3 reminds me, "Give ear to my words, O Lord, Consider my groaning. Heed the sound of my cry for help, my King and my God, For to Thee do I pray. In the morning, O Lord, Thou wilt hear my voice; In the morning I will order my prayer to Thee and eagerly watch."

When I am focused on Christ as my example, poise can be reflected in my life as I confidently confront issues on a daily basis and as I fulfill my responsibility as a Christian leader.

1. Consider the "poise" of Christ. What Scripture can you identify that validates His poise especially when confronted by the high priests, the Pharisees and Pilate?
2. What can you learn from Christ's poise related to your own personal or professional life?
3. What are some of the areas that get you off balance? What could help you remain poised?
4. What kind of leader are you within your organization or team as it relates to poise? How would your employer and/or peers rate you?
5. Do a personal inventory of your own poise and how well you are remaining balanced. Seek out godly counsel and advice from those who can help speak truth to you in love (Ephesians 4:15).

This week, write out and memorize Luke 2:52.

REASONABLENESS

REASONABLENESS: Having a sound mind by being level headed, sane and demonstrating common sense.

Are we at the point in the coverage of professional sports where we need to delay broadcasts in order to bleep out profanities in live postgame network TV interviews? More and more we get a regular dose of obscenities from athletes and coaches who share their joys and frustrations with the fans. Football analyst Paul Maguire commented after one episode, "These people are very excited. I don't think anything was done intentionally to embarrass or hurt anybody. I think they didn't even realize they said something offensive." But they should have, says former player Phil Simms, who also broadcasts NFL games. "It bothered a lot of people. I've been there. I know it's such an emotional game. But you have to know you're talking to an audience when they stick out a microphone. You can't let that happen. And it's absolutely the obligation of the players—you do owe something to the public."

1. What does it mean to think before you speak or act? Why is this important for an athlete or coach to consider?
2. What roles do common sense and reasoning skills play in your sport or your job?

We live in a world that seems to have abandoned common sense and reason. Newspapers and television continually highlight individuals who have made irrational and irresponsible choices. Numerous examples include stories of people who drink and drive, men and women who lead sexually active lifestyles outside of their marriage and those who engage in illegal activity, breaking the laws of the land. Sadly, these examples are regularly reported about both Christians and non-Christians. We often wonder what those people were thinking prior to their illogical decisions. I would assert that they have lost their ability to reason, which is directly oppositional to God's will for us.

We may be educationally and technologically advanced, but many of us struggle at home, in our sports and in the workplace because we pursue intelligence but lack common sense. Proverbs 16:9 reminds us, however, that "The mind of a man plans his way, but the Lord directs his step." If we heed this proverb and additional urging from Jesus to "come, let us reason together," we will let God direct our steps, not society.

Naysayers of the church claim that Christianity promotes blind acceptance rather than reason, but nothing could be further from the truth. Christianity is the one religion which demands the continuous and daring development of the intellect. As Christians we are to utilize scripture to guide our decisions and actions, not our prejudices or self-centered wisdom.

The distractions of life either pull us away or draw us closer to the goal of godly reason. Using our minds as we address and try to answer the hard questions of life seems simple and easy to do, but there are many people, including Christians, who do not. Many men and women blindly walk through life seeking answers to life but sadly, they settle for false truth in their peers and the secular world around them. Their belief system is based on the going fads or worse yet, whatever makes them feel good. They pursue truth that doesn't hurt or offend them. They pursue truth which supports their ungodly lifestyle and they accept truth that doesn't make them feel guilty.

Sadly, these individuals are missing the mark on what it means to truly live because they have not taken the time to seek the real meaning of life as found in the Bible. Jesus promises life this way:

- I came that they might have life and have it more abundantly
- I am the resurrection and the life
- I am the way, the truth and the life

Bottom line: Jesus wants his children to live. These verses give us the idea of his mission. Jefferson said it this way, "People everywhere want to live, but the tragedy is they don't succeed. There is a path which leads to life, but there are only a few who find it. We do the very things which curtail the capacity for living, drying up the springs of vitality. We imitate the bad habits and methods of others. We become cowards allowing ourselves to be hoodwinked, browbeaten and cheated of our birthright. We allow greed and the security of this world to steal our heart, losing sight of the richest satisfactions which only Christ can bring. We settle for immediate gratification forsaking the treasures of future years. Our life isn't full or rich or sweet because we are handicapped by our doubts and fears, enslaved to the unreasonable standards and requirements of this foolish world."

1. Share examples of people you know or heard of who have exhibited common sense and reasoning skills in their daily living.
2. Do you feel like you are really living based on the quote from Jefferson?
3. Christianity is a religion based on facts and using your mind. How is this different from other religions?

Recently I met with a man who struggled greatly with godly reason versus societal influence. He had heard me speak on 1 Corinthians 15:17 which says, "and if Christ has not been raised, your faith is worthless; you are still in your sins." He was bothered by this statement. In fact, he was distraught because he admitted for the first time he had no answers for his existence. Though he claimed to be a Christian, he had no belief system, and the little faith he did have wasn't in God but in the world. He admitted never taking the time to think with his mind about what he believes and does not believe. Instead, he had allowed his peers and the world to think and reason for him. I encouraged him to open God's Word and search the scripture for truth. Now, he is committed to beginning the journey to discover God's purposes for his life through Jesus Christ.

To expose the folly of men, Jesus continually asked questions forcing people to think and exercise reason. Jesus' Sermon on the Mount, found in Matthew 5-7, is a classic expression of practical common sense with remarks on a number of different subjects including the irrationality associated with profanity, his disgust with repetitious prayers and meaningless fasting, and whether or not it was appropriate to do anything on the Sabbath.

Profanity is a sin against reason because it reveals the soul of a fool by being utterly senseless. Rather than thinking through an appropriate response, profanity does not reveal level headedness. The use of profane language does not show reasonableness.

Jesus also shares in this sermon his insight on repetitious prayers. The religious leaders of his day repeated pious words on the street corners, being satisfied with their neighbors' gaze. To Jesus such devotion was ridiculous. For fasting to have value it must be an exercise of the soul, not a mechanical duty. It isn't the abstinence from food which is pleasing to God, but the condition of the heart of the person who is doing the fasting. Jesus urged people to pray to God and fast in secret with a sincere heart.

One institution held in high reverence for the Jews was the Sabbath. The day was so revered it degenerated into slavery. It was made so holy you could barely even move or breathe without breaking the laws. That wasn't reasonable. Jesus saw through the maze of man made laws and shed light and life upon the situation. He said, "The Sabbath was made for man and not man for the Sabbath." The life of man is the first consideration. Therefore, it was lawful to do good on the Sabbath and to set men free from bondage of unreasonableness.

Jesus' message is that the Father is eager to give his children everything in abundance. Jesus urges people to be sensible at every turn, using the mind God has given us. If you want to understand the Christian life, open up your Bible and your mind. If you desire to know the truth, then live it. This is how you can have a sound mind and gain common sense. You can never become a fully devoted follower of Christ or a successful leader or manager until you commit to these disciplines in the workplace, and most importantly, in your life and family.

1. Define "reasonableness" in the context of your sport and in life.
2. Identify the specific passages in Matthew 5-7 where Jesus discusses reasonable behavior related to swearing, praying, fasting and the Sabbath. Does he address any other subjects beyond these four areas?
3. Why does Jesus challenge us to use our minds?
4. What is the impact for you personally and for your team when you demonstrate "reasonableness" during your daily tasks and responsibilities?
5. How did you establish your belief system? Can you articulate what you believe to another person? If so, share your beliefs with the rest of the group.

This week, write out and memorize Proverbs 16:9.

REVERENCE

REVERENCE: Giving honor where it is due and respecting the possessions and property of others.

Roberto Alomar made a terrible mistake several years ago when he became enraged at umpire John Hirschbeck and ended it by spitting on him. Alomar was vilified coast to coast by all of baseball including teammates, league officials and fans. Alomar told Sports Illustrated, "I'm not a bad person. I care about my family. I care about my kids. I'm from a good family. I made a mistake. God knows I didn't mean anything bad." His outburst was a surprise to those who knew him. Teammate Mark Parent said, "He's not a monster. He doesn't have a rap sheet. I've known him and his family since he was 17. He's a nice kid from a great family. His parents taught him the right and wrong way. Now people think he's Ty Cobb." Three days after Alomar spit on Hirschbeck he issued a public apology and pledged $50,000 to a foundation that fights a rare disease that Hirschbeck's son died of in 1993.

1. What is your initial reaction to the word "reverence"?
2. Why is reverence an important character quality?

If a person never offends in word or deed he is perfect. Obviously, none of us qualifies—not even a good kid like Roberto Alomar. Should we be shocked at Alomar's outburst? No.

By nature we aren't reverent. Our sinful flesh seeks to serve ourselves and not God, and it appears our nation is becoming less and less reverent as the years go by. Older people lament that the younger generation isn't as respectful as they were. In many instances, society has banished most forms of reverence. While many people display cleverness and brilliance, they lack an upward reach to God. Their talk is often witty and mocking at the expense of high and sacred things. While claiming to be believers, they lack reverence. Even in our modern day churches, the house of God is often treated like a sports arena or a tavern.

Many times I have observed "irreverence" in action. Occasionally it is watching people flippantly enter the church building or by inappropriate clothes worn to church. I have also seen it prior to weddings and funerals in people who mock the presence of God. Even on the ball fields, I have witnessed players pointing to the heavens as if to thank God and then stealing the glory of God through their subsequent words and behavior.

To show reverence means to "respect, regard, esteem and honor." It reflects multiple attitudes of awe, fear and adoration, with an abiding consciousness of dependence on God. The phrase "fear of the Lord" is a good way of capturing it. The wise men of Israel were convinced that the fear of the Lord is the beginning of wisdom (Proverbs 1:7). They wanted to make men conscious of the existence of a God of infinite power, wisdom and goodness. He is the High and Holy One who inhabits eternity and therefore should not be approached carelessly or thought of lightly.

The temple in Jerusalem was built to establish the fear of the Lord in the hearts of the people. The architecture, specifically designed by God, was a continual reminder of the need to be reverent. The truth was proclaimed that God was majestic and holy and could be approached only by a humble and prostrate heart. Likewise today, you can't be reverent in selective moments. God calls us to be reverent at all times or not at all. Instead this attitude must run through every vein in our body. Jefferson stated, "It (reverence) is a settled habit of the spirit, a fixed attitude of the heart and an unchanging trend of all the currents of the being toward God. No matter what Jesus is saying or doing, we feel we are in the presence of a reverential man."

Jesus' reverence for the temple in Jerusalem was well known. Every stone in it spoke to him of God, and every ceremony celebrated within its courts reflected God's plan and purposes. Any desecration of a building erected to promote God's glory was to him horrible. The temple was a place for eyes to be opened and hearts cleansed. The temple was indeed a holy place to Jesus. But Jesus' countrymen cared nothing for God or his temple. They converted the temple courts into a market place and drowned the anthems and prayers with the clink of money and the bellowing of animals. Finally, one day Jesus had enough and cleansed the temple. To the onlookers it might have looked like an avenging fury, but he reminded them that this was his Father's house built for God's glory. The temple was intended to be a refuge for God's people. Jesus' cleansing of the temple pierced the merchants and bystanders like a dagger.

1. Share examples where you have seen "irreverent" and "reverent" behavior. Why did you classify your examples in these terms?
2. Read Luke 19:45-48 and John 2:13-16. Why did the desecration of the temple anger Jesus? Why was his response an appropriate course of action?
3. How can reverence be applied to your daily life?

Jesus' reverence went beyond the temple. In the Lord's Prayer, his opening line is "hallowed be thy name." It is mentioned at the forefront of the prayer to remind ourselves to place our eyes completely on God. He asks us to put God first in our lives because he always put God first himself. His supreme ambition was for his Father's name to be kept beautiful and holy. He told his disciples, "When you pray, pray that God's name may be consecrated, reverenced and kept holy." He urges us to live life to the total glory of God, and to speak, act and live so others might see our good works and glorify the Father in heaven.

The religious leaders of Jesus' day tried to appear reverent but their hearts were shallow. They revered forms of worship like prayer and fasting rituals, but their attitudes revealed their true motives. Jesus urged people to worship God in "spirit and in truth" but worship without the spirit of reverence becomes empty and meaningless. Jefferson said, "The Pharisees worship had cut out the spirit of adoration. It was cut and dried, dead, mechanical, without a heart and without a soul. Reverence is beautiful in all of its expressions. When reverence dies, reverence becomes corpse like and it contaminates all who handle it."

Jesus' reverence for his Father extended also to the things God created. Therefore, nothing was treated irreverently, dragged down into vulgarity or converted into a joke. It would be inconceivable for Jesus to act irreverently yet so many believers totally contradict Jesus' example.

This moral collapse and failure may be in part due to our familiarity with the ways of God, taking off the edge of our sensibility and our fear of the Lord. In other cases, the lines between decency (right) and indecency (wrong) have grown gray.

I believe we have lost our sense of awe and respect of God. To a certain degree, we may be ashamed of being afraid of anybody or anything, including God. Fear is one of the elements of reverence and there is a perception that all fear, including a healthy fear of the Lord, is degrading. Fear is categorized into two ways: godly fear and a fear which is ungodly. The right fear of God cleanses people.

Finally, we are told in Scripture that we (the Body of Christ) are the temple. 1 Corinthians says, "you are God's temple and God's spirit lives in you" (3:16-17) and later we read, "your body is a temple of the Holy Spirit, who is in you" (6:19). God's message to us is that each one of us has been bought with a price through the blood of Jesus Christ. Just as God is revered through the temple, we need to revere God through our body as well.

How can we become reverent? First of all, I implore you to consider the words of Proverbs 1:7. A healthy fear of God will bring wisdom, hope and peace. Second, ask yourself this question when faced with choices throughout the day: "What would Jesus do?" Evaluate your response in light of how you believe Jesus would respond. Third, consider placing God at the forefront of every conversation and activity you engage in. Make him first....you won't be disappointed.

1. Discuss what it means to have a healthy "fear of the Lord?" How does having this fear change your behavior?
2. How does maintaining a spirit of reverence help you be an effective witness for Christ at work or at play?
3. How can a believer in Christ keep from falling into a meaningless and empty reverence like the Pharisees?
4. Read 1 Corinthians 3:16-17 and 6:19-20. How do you react when you hear you are the temple?
5. Re-read the last paragraph in this study and reflect on the benefits associated with putting these three points into practice. Do you agree that you won't be disappointed? Why or why not?

This week, write out and memorize Proverbs 1:7.

SINCERITY

SINCERITY: Endeavoring to do what is right, without ulterior motives.

Mickey Mantle's teammates filled a large church in Dallas, Texas to witness the funeral of a sporting hero and national icon. One member of this team had been with Mantle during his last days. Mantle may have jokingly called Bobby Richardson a "milk drinker" in their Yankee days, but Mantle had never flaunted his escapades or used foul language around the born-again Christian who lockered nearby. The former second baseman, now a lay preacher, recalled sharing his faith with Mantle a few times when they were with the Yankees, only to detect "a fear of death, an emptiness he tried to cover with harmful choices." Years later, when Mantle knew he was losing his fight with cancer, Mantle called Richardson asking him to pray with him over the telephone. In the days prior to his death, Richardson was asked to come to Dallas. Mickey said, "Bobby, I want you to know I've accepted Christ as my Savior." Richardson discovered Mantle had been listening to him many years earlier, although it had not seemed so at the time.

1. What are some examples of Christian athletes showing their faith in public? How did people respond?
2. Describe what happens in a relationship when sincerity is present. How about when it's lacking?

Recently I participated in the affirmation time of a group of men who attend a weekly Bible study. The facilitator of this process gave a few ground rules to set the stage, including, "Your comments must be genuine and heartfelt." He wasn't looking for trite phrases but words which were well thought out and accurately reflected our feelings. In essence, he desired for us to be sincere. Sincerity means that you endeavor to do what is right, without ulterior motives.

Sincerity is an indispensable trait demanded in our relationships. It is impossible to be a true friend if sincerity is lacking. In other words, it's not possible to be an "insincere friend;" it's a flat contradiction. Mike Yaconelli once said, "Pretending is the grease of non-relationships." We can rely on sincere people 24 hours a day, every day, but when we look for sincerity in others and don't find it, we are grieved and disappointed.

Sincerity is a virtue which the human heart instinctively craves. It is the keystone in the arch, and without it the arch collapses. Parents seek this quality in their children. Though a child may follow the parent's instructions, it means far more when they see their actions performed with the simplicity of a sincere heart. Jefferson tells us "sincerity" is the queen of all the character virtues and all the remaining character qualities are children of the queen.

In the secular community, insincerity is common. Sadly, Christians mimic the world's lead, as many of us are indistinguishable from unbelievers in our conduct. Every day we face opportunities to do right or wrong and many times our sincerity, or lack of it, is revealed. We live in a world full of trickery, dishonesty and deceit. Even in Jefferson's era, almost 100 years ago, he remarked, "Businesses are cursed with dishonesty, the political world abounds in duplicity and there is sham, pretense and humbuggery everywhere." If the times were perilous in the early 1900's, what would Jefferson say about our 21st century? The bottom line is we live in a society where dishonesty abounds. Jefferson's words still ring true today, "We say things which we do not mean, express emotions which we do not feel, we praise when we secretly condemn, we smile when there is a frown on the face of the heart, we give compliments when we are really thinking curses, striving a hundred times a week to make people think we are other than we are." Many things are attained through half truths or outright lies. What is the penalty for our misspoken words and deeds? Does the reality of condemnation before Almighty God stir us to right behaviors?

It is a sad, deceitful and demoralized world we find ourselves living in, but thank God there are some people upon whom we can depend. Many times these people are out of the limelight but as you get to know them, you find they are trustworthy. Others may be more prominent, but there is an overriding spirit of service which emerges, indicating their true humility. We test these relationships and discover they are true. Sincerity isn't gaudy, it doesn't glitter and it has no sparkle....but it is substantial and it is life giving. It sustains and nurtures the soul.

1. Is it possible to be a true friend without sincerity? Why or why not?
2. Would people describe you as sincere? Why or why not?
3. What is more important: To tell people about your faith or to live your faith out in front of them?

Sincerity in its loveliest form is found in Jesus Christ. He was incapable of telling a lie. Nothing stirred his wrath more than to be with people who pretended to be what they were not. He could spot the hypocrites, and he wasn't afraid to speak harsh words directly to them. Jesus used plain words when speaking to the Pharisees and Sadducees when he called them "liars, murderers and hypocrites." It was the sincerity of Jesus which drove him into deadly conflict with them. Jesus exhorted people to speak the truth, urging them to let their "yes be yes" and their "no be no." To Jesus, a man's word was his bond, his oath before God.

One day Jesus told the crowd they were of their father the devil and they were eager to follow the lusts of his evil ways. It was plain, direct speech spoken with sincerity of truth. Had he kept silent or pretended to be ignorant it would have meant he was a liar himself. He was unswervingly loyal to the truth. Even the warnings of Jesus to those on their way to hell were delivered with total sincerity. It would have been far crueler for Jesus to not speak the truth than to tell them exactly the consequences of their words and actions.

With the woman at the well, Jesus accurately spoke words of truth, penetrating her with his tactful questions. Jesus knew exactly how to best communicate his message to each specific individual.

He called the leaders in Jerusalem liars, blind men, fools, serpents and vipers. Jesus was accurately informing them of their pitiful condition. What else could a sincere friend do? There was not a trace of bitterness in Jesus' language. It was the calm statement of a horrible fact. The Lord of truth must of necessity use words which accurately characterize the persons who are to be instructed and warned. Before Pilate, Jesus uttered his declaration that he had come into the world to bear witness to the truth. This was his work and he never shirked it. Though people lied about him, misrepresenting his deeds, words and motives, he stood calm and radiant.

Jesus holds nothing back. He tones nothing down--he exaggerates nothing. He declares all things as they are. His character is revealed in his speech. His words are simply the truth. A man like this can be a refuge in the time of storm. When we are weary and heavy laden, we can rest our souls upon one who is faithful. The voices of this world are difficult to trust, but his voice inspires assurance and quenches uncertainty and doubt. What he teaches about God we can receive. What he tells us of the soul we can depend upon. What he asserts concerning the principles of a victorious life, we can act upon, never doubting. When he tells us to do a thing we can do it: we can be assured it is the best thing to do. When he warns us against a course of action, we can shun it knowing in that direction lies death.

In our workplace, church and family, Jesus exhorts us to take the path of sincerity with boldness. Years ago, I had a friend at work who spoke encouraging words, but I didn't value the words because I sensed insincerity. Ultimately I discovered his words were not true and to this day, it is difficult to trust him due to the disconnect between words and reality. Jesus urged us to "speak the truth in love" and when done appropriately, it is a gift we can give to those with whom we work or live.

Today, I invite you to pray asking God to give you the character quality of sincerity. To communicate truth in a genuine, authentic way just as Jesus modeled it for us. Our souls will be at peace as we experience the same calmness and satisfaction that comes through living a sincere life.

1. Read Matthew 5:13-16. How does this verse apply to sincerity?
2. What can we learn from Jesus' examples of sincerity as noted above?
3. How can you become sincere in your daily routine?

This week, write out and memorize Matthew 5:16.

STRENGTH

STRENGTH: Having power, force and vigor for the task assigned.

As Ed Barreto crossed the finish line in 5 hours and 32 minutes in the Upstate Marathon in 1991, it was the end of much more than a 26.2 mile run. Barreto, age 54, had run 75 marathons that year breaking the world record by one. Baretto commented afterwards, "My knees are in bad shape and I'm all burned out." I would say Baretto has amazing strength. Can you imagine the physical stamina and mental toughness it must have taken for him to run 75 marathons in a year? Not to mention the fact that he was 54 years old when he did it!! You can bet there were days when he must have wanted to call it quits but he didn't, and he ultimately achieved his goal.

1. Describe the greatest act of physical strength you've ever seen or personally experienced? Where did the strength come from to accomplish this feat?
2. Describe the greatest act of mental strength you've ever seen or personally experienced? Where did the strength come from to accomplish this feat?

Last year I saw "Team Extreme" in action. This group of bodybuilders work for Youth With A Mission and they put on quite a show as they blow up hot water bottles, bend bars of steel, crush full cans of pop and tear up entire phone books. Their message is to help people see physical feats of strength and then compare those feats to the strength of Jesus Christ. From an outsider's point of view, this may seem like a strange comparison, but it is a very effective and powerful message. While we can visibly appreciate physical strength, what does it mean to have true strength found only in Christ?

The people of Palestine did not fully recognize, understand or appreciate Jesus Christ or his strength while he was with them. When you picture Jesus, what stands out? What about those who saw Jesus first hand? What were the first impressions Jesus made upon his contemporaries? In the first chapter of his book, Mark reveals four different events and the impact Jesus made upon each of them:

1. Jesus' baptism – John the Baptist recognized he was "unworthy" (1:1-13)
2. Men fishing in the boat – four of them left all they had to follow Jesus (1:14-20)
3. Synagogue teaching – Jesus taught with authority and the people were amazed (1:21-28)
4. Healing the sick – people gathered all around Jesus (1:29-34)

In these four examples, we see the first impression Jesus made on the people was a combination of authority, power and leadership. Bottom line: The teaching of the Gospels illustrates the strength of Jesus. The strength wasn't in his physical prowess, but instead it was in the strength of his character. He attracted people. Wherever he went, to the seashore, hilltop, desert or city, he was surrounded by crowds. Only a man of great strength of character can attract the masses. Not only did Jesus draw crowds but he stirred their souls whenever they came near him. Consider Nicodemus (John 3:1-21) and the Roman centurion (Matthew 27:54) as examples.

Nicodemus was one of the leading officials of his day. He came to Jesus in the evening with many questions. Their conversation challenged Nicodemus to re-think his whole perspective on living. Though we don't necessarily know if he was converted that night, we are led to believe this encounter radically changed his entire life. In the same way, the Roman centurion knew Jesus was who he claimed to be based on what he saw first hand at the foot of the cross. Jesus profoundly impacted people.

How about the Romans? What impression did they have about Jesus? When they came to arrest him in the Garden of Gethsemane, they asked if he was indeed Jesus of Nazareth. Jesus responded "I am," and they fell backward on the ground. When Jesus stood before Pilate, we see the fear of Pilate. He was afraid of Jesus, wringing his hands in uncertainty, washing his hands and trying to get rid of this man. The strength of Jesus' character poured out and it frightened him.

1. The spiritual life of a Christian is much more like a marathon run than a sprint. What kind of strength do you need to run a marathon race?

2. Based on the reactions of people in Mark 1:1-34 and other Scripture, how did Jesus reveal his strength of character? Why were people drawn to his strength?
3. Describe a time when you had to persevere. How did you get through?

When you think about it, we know very little about the life of Jesus Christ as recorded in the four Gospels. The writers deal with only three of the 33 years of his life, and tell us less than 40 days out of those three years. Even in those 40 days we only catch brief glimpses of the story. Compared to other writings of famous people, it would be difficult to write a complete biography on Christ.

It is obvious the goal of Matthew, Mark, Luke and John was to write something entirely different than a biography. The writers did not tell us about his stature, the clothes he wore or the houses he lived in. We know very little about him prior to thirty years of age. He held no political office or in a church. He did not grow up wealthy. He was born in a stable, worked in a carpenter's shop, taught for three years and then died on a cross. Apart from a few recorded miracles and a brutal crucifixion, his life could be summarized as uneventful.

Jefferson said it this way, "We are driven to the conclusion that they were writing not the biography of Jesus but the character of Jesus." The stories told in the New Testament reveal the character of Jesus, revealing his heart and soul, and thus we can know him better than anyone who has ever lived upon the earth.

Some people may say, "Jesus lived 2,000 years ago, and therefore you cannot be sure about his character." According to Jefferson this is wrong thinking, "You can understand a great man better at a distance than when standing near him. No truly great man is ever appreciated at his worth by the people in the midst of whom he lives." For example, the world did not appreciate Abraham Lincoln until he died. Today we understand Luther far better than his peers. Likewise, we are able to evaluate the strength of Jesus' character better today because we see the impact of his life over the past 2,000 years.

Jesus' power and strength are reference to his omniscience (infinite knowledge), his omnipotence (infinite power) and his omnipresence (present everywhere at the same time). Each of these words reveals his strength. There is absolutely nothing he cannot do. The words of Paul in Philippians 4:13 is a great encouragement, "I can do all things through Christ who strengthens me." It is Christ's power which equips us to handle any situation.

Jesus' strength dared to reverse all human standards, it confounded the wise and it made all things new. According to Jefferson, "His ideas had the force of dynamite and his personality the power to change human hearts." He pulled down strongholds of iniquity and established righteousness and peace on the earth. Jesus draws people to himself, infuses them with a new spirit and sends them back out into the world to make a difference for the Kingdom. Jefferson said, "It is by the changing of the character of a man that we change the character of other men, and by changing the character of many men we change the character of institutions and ultimately of empires and civilizations."

The greatest proof of Jesus' strength is found in the intensity of the hatred and love which he provoked. Jefferson said, "Just as Jesus drove some people to hate him, he drove others to love him. He kindled a devotion superior to anything ever known." His impact went beyond Bethlehem, Nazareth and Jerusalem. All of the remaining eleven disciples, except for John, suffered a martyr's death. Countless persecution and sufferings have been heaped upon those who have proclaimed Christ as their Savior. Today, he is still making a radical difference in the lives of men and women around the world, giving them strength to fulfill God's plans and purposes.

Remember, when you are faced with an impossible situation and you feel like giving up, rely on the strength and character of Jesus Christ. You have a choice. You can choose to gut out the spiritual race on your own and burn out, or you can choose to depend on His power and finish the race with a big kick.

1. Besides Jesus Christ, what other Bible characters showed tremendous strength, power and determination in a trying situation?
2. What modern day examples come to mind of someone displaying great strength of character?
3. Can we really do everything through Christ who gives us strength? Why did you answer the question this way?
4. How can you remember to rely on God's strength, rather than your weakness?

This week, write out and memorize Philippians 4:13.

TRUST

TRUST: Believing completely and totally in someone or something.

Figure skating is usually regarded as a highly individual sport--one athlete, one pair of skates and one rink. But it takes partnership, cooperation and understanding to succeed in pairs skating. Olympic skaters agree that you must worry about both yourself and your partner at the same time, unlike a singles event where you're concerned only about yourself. The bottom line about pairs skating might have been said best by former Olympic skater, Sandra Bezic. She said, "Pairs skating is like joining two puddles of water. You link them, let them fill in and form one balanced pool." In other words, pairs skating is all about teamwork and trust.

1. Have you ever been let down by someone? Ever thought you were going to make the team, but were cut instead? Or have you shared something in complete confidence only to learn your confidence was betrayed? How about a friend who offered to help with a project and then bailed out? Describe how you feel when someone breaks your trust.
2. Each of these scenarios destroys trust, but what exactly is trust?

I recently spoke with a church leader whose trustworthiness had been challenged, and rightly so. He had a pattern of being late to meetings and many times was missing entirely with questionable excuses. It was perceived he wasn't working because he was often away from his office, and those he supervised were complaining about his lack of leadership. This man clearly needed to work on rebuilding trust with many people. If we are brutally honest with ourselves, many of us can probably identify at least one person in our lives with whom we need to build trust.

As we pursue trust, let us first consider Jesus Christ. A key question to ponder is: "Where do we put our trust?" Jesus' enemies at the crucifixion mocked him saying, "He trusts in God" (Matthew 27:43). In this simple statement, Jesus' deadliest foes gave testimony of his deep trust in His Father. Jesus' strength and gladness came from his steadfast trust. At age 12, he told his mother, "I must be about my Father's business." On the cross, he said, "Father into your hands I commit my spirit." From the beginning to the end, Jesus' trust in God was never broken.

What happens to us when horrific experience rocks our trust? Does our faith in God overcome the intense pain? Are we so dazed that we can't even see God? Many things work to blot out our trust. Discouragement may, or unfulfilled dreams and ambitions. Disappointments, persecutions, misunderstandings, hostilities, failures....many people are overcome by them. Where is God in times of trouble? Pastor and author Bruce Larson says that he grew up saying yes to biblical doctrines, but eventually he sensed that God was asking him deeper questions:

1. Will you trust me with your life? Yes or no?
2. Will you entrust yourself to my church family? Yes or no?
3. Will you serve me by getting involved with others? Yes or no?

Jesus' trust in God allowed him to say yes to each of these questions. No matter what he faced he said, "Thy will be done." Defeat itself could not daunt him or make him draw back. If we desire to be trustworthy, we must begin by having resolute trust in God and in God alone. just like Jesus Christ.

1. Which sports require the greatest amount of trust among teammates in order to be successful?
2. In what ways have you seen trust work? What happens when there is a lack of trust?

3. What are some of the obstacles that stop "us" from trusting completely in God? Why is it hard to trust God?

We build trust with others each time we choose:

- Integrity over image – committing to be the right person and do the right thing. An arrogant ego makes us untrustworthy.
- Truth over convenience – committing to speak the truth instead of half truths or white lies.
- Love over personal gain – committing to serve others rather than serving ourselves.

PepsiCo Chairman and CEO Craig Weatherup explains it this way, "You don't build trust by talking about it. You build it by achieving results, always with integrity and in a manner that shows real personal regard for the people with whom you work."

Two pillars make trust possible: integrity and love. In our daily lives, we confidently trust God because he completely fulfills both. Likewise, when an individual or organization demonstrates integrity by keeping commitments, sharing the truth, and truly loving you, trust follows. Trust is the glue for all healthy relationships and keeps us on track. Machiavelli argues that fear is more controlling than love or its derivatives; however, fear simply compels behavior, it does not promote trustworthiness. Dr. Richard M. Biery tells us, "Where fear does not reach, trust can. Organizations are too complex and our individual liberties too strong to successfully govern for long by fear."

During a recent presentation, I spoke on "trust" and used the following illustration to test these two pillars. I blindfolded two volunteers, one of whom knew me well; the other was a complete stranger. After they were blindfolded I placed a chair in front of them and asked each to step on the chair, place both of his arms over his chest and fall backwards upon my command. I claimed that I would catch them just before they fell. Without hesitation, both fell backwards into the arms of a number of men who had silently positioned themselves behind the chairs. Later, both men commented that they were willing to fall because of the perception of integrity and love they sensed from me. This was surprising, especially from the person who didn't know me at all. However, he said he was comfortable doing so because he had heard me speak on the value of character.

Trust is built through the belief that God knows what is best for your life. God simply asks us to trust him in keeping his promises. He asks us to let go of reasons, rights, and fears and simply throw our arms around him. As our trust and dependence upon him deepen, and as we grow in our integrity and love, we will become trustworthy in our daily lives. Are you up to the challenge? God will be glorified as you pursue this vital character quality.

1. Read Matthew 17:14-20. What does this story tell us about trusting God?
2. What is the evidence of a life that trusts God?
3. When it comes to building trust, do you need more integrity or more love? Why?
4. Who is someone you trust? Why?
5. Do you consider yourself trustworthy? Why or why not?

This week, write out and memorize Psalm 56:11.

FCA

FELLOWSHIP OF CHRISTIAN ATHLETES

FCA's VISION

To see the world impacted for Jesus Christ through the influence of athletes and coaches.

FCA's MISSION

To present to athletes and coaches, and all whom they influence the challenge and adventure of receiving Jesus Christ as Savior and Lord, serving Him in their relationships and in the fellowship of the Church.

FCA MINISTRIES FUNDAMENTALS

FCA Ministry Fundamentals are Share Him, Seek Him, Lead Others and Love Others. The Ministry Fundamentals are the simple expression of what we are trying to accomplish. They are the foundations of all we do as a ministry.

We believe that healthy, loving relationships (Love Others) are also critical whether it is with family and friends or within the Church of Christ Simply put our Fundamentals can be defied as:

• Share Him: The Fellowship of Christian Athletes desires to share Jesus with those who do not have a personal relationship with Him. We believe that salvation is only found in Jesus, and with great passion we desire to share this with the world.

• Seek Him: The Fellowship of Christian Athletes desires to assist those who have a relationship with Jesus in seeking Him. A life-long pursuit of knowing and loving Jesus is not complicated, but it takes effort and diligence.

• Lead Others: The Fellowship of Christian Athletes desires to equip those who have found a personal faith in Christ to actively lead others in the pursuit of Jesus.

• Love Others: The Fellowship of Christian Athletes realizes that the most powerful force in the world is love. We desire to be obedient to the Lord as He said that we would be known by our love.

CSRM

- CSRM is an organization that helps Sports and Recreation Ministers in the local church reach the world for Christ.
- CSRM is an organization that facilitates a network of sports and recreation ministry professionals within the world-wide church of Christ.
- CSRM is Christ centered, Biblically based, evangelistically focused, international in scope and ecumenical in participation.

History - CSRM began in 1995, emerging from a grass roots movement in the early 90's. It was created to provide a professional organization for those seeking to use sports and recreation as a tool for evangelism and discipleship within the local church. It has since been incorporated as a 501(c)(3) and currently serves over 700 churches.

Membership - CSRM members can be found in countries from around the world and its membership is open to any sports and recreation minister whose ministry is based in a local church; any person training current or future sports ministers and to other non-voting supporting members.

Conferences - CSRM sponsors an annual conference at a local church for anyone interested in sport and recreation ministry. In addition CSRM has also developed an international network of regional conferences being held in different cities in different countries. For the latest conferencing information access the CSRM website at www.csrm.org

Journal - CSRM publishes a quarterly journal. "The Sports Minister" keeps our membership up to date with training options, conference information, regional gatherings and job opportunities. It also serves as a repository of cutting edge research, programming ideas, past and current sports ministry history and all CSRM business.

AIA

AIA is a global pioneer, innovator and servant leader in sport ministry

OUR VISION

Helping fulfill the great commission by Taking the initiative to share the gospel with 1 billion people annually through the platform of sport (exposure) Giving 100 million people annually the opportunity to individually receive Jesus Christ (evangelism) Building a global movement of 15,000 spiritually mature athletic influencers by 2008 (discipleship)

OUR MISSION

Athletes in Action exists to boldly proclaim the love and truth of Jesus Christ to those uniquely impacted by sport worldwide by winning, building, and sending athletic influencers.

OUR VALUES

FAITH - Now faith is being sure of what we hope for and certain of what we do not see. (Hebrews 11:1, NIV)

Believing God to transform our own lives through a deeper and more intimate connection with Him, the lives of those to whom we minister, and the millions we are trying to influence. Trusting God for that which only HE can accomplish!

FAMILY - Each one should use whatever gift he has received to serve others, faithfully administering God?s grace in its various forms. (I Peter 4:10,NIV)

Connecting through meaningful partnerships including other CCC ministries, churches, LIFE partners, and other ministries. Building a multi-cultural community reflecting God?s heart for people from all nations, tribes, and tongues.

Encouraging the development of strong godly families and marriages among our staff, LIFE partners, and disciples.

FCA

Fellowship of Christian Athletes
8701 Leeds Road
Kansas City, MO 64129
1-800-289-0909
www.FCA.org

CSRM

Church Sports and Recreation Ministers
C/O The World Outreach Center
5350 Broadmoor Circle NW
Canton, Ohio 44709
330-493-4824 office, 330-493-0852 fax
www.csrm.org

AIA

Athletes in Action
651 Taylor Drive
Xenia, OH 45385
937-352-1000
937-352-1001 (fax)
www.aia.com
athletesinaction@aia.com